Practical Suggestions for Teaching

Edited by Alice Miel

———◆·◆———

Helping Children in Oral Communication

TITLES IN THIS SERIES

HELPING CHILDREN

in

ORAL COMMUNICATION

———◆———

Alberta Munkres

Professor Emeritus, School of Education
University of Denver

Assisted by Denver Public School Teachers:

LaRue Benesh, *Sherman Elementary School*
Alberta M. Jesser, *Whiteman Elementary School*
John W. Low, *Swansea Elementary School*
Montford S. Whiteley, *Palmer Elementary School*

BUREAU OF PUBLICATIONS

Teachers College, Columbia University • New York • 1959

Editor's Introduction

SOME OF THE MOST TROUBLESOME QUESTIONS FACING TEACHERS CLUSTER around best ways to help children learn effective and correct oral language expression. Teachers wonder how to encourage the silent ones, and how to help the ramblers and the ones who are halting and awkward in talking before an audience. They wonder what to do about boring reports and they are not certain when and how they should point out errors.

Although Dr. Munkres has not set out to attack singly and directly such specific questions, abundant, concrete help on these and other matters is to be found in every paragraph. The author has organized her material around five aspects of oral communication—conversing and discussing, storytelling, reporting and making speeches, dramatizing, and one which cuts across the other four, namely, using words well.

In each section a pattern is followed. First comes the presentation of an example—a real conversation, discussion, story, or report —as transcribed from a tape. Second, there is an explanation of the teaching efforts which led up to this oral product. Third, the author adds comments and raises questions to help the reader in examining the decisions made by the teacher involved and in thinking about alternatives. The booklet is especially helpful in showing how seemingly the same assignment may allow all pupils to produce according to their own potentialities and how each child can have experiences in oral expression without causing others to lose opportunity or attention. The use of small groups in preparation for presentation to a larger audience is described at a number of points.

All these potential helps are incorporated in a functional way within a solid argument for careful planning and teaching in the area of oral communication.

ALICE MIEL

How true it is
That all will know
A man, by speech betrayed;
Though few may guess,
And fewer care,
How much he reads,
How well he writes.

How fine it is
To read and write
As ably as one can;
But, oh, the need
Of everyone,
To learn the art
Of talking well!

Preface

BUT, OH, THE NEED OF EVERYONE, TO LEARN THE ART OF TALKING WELL!
Acceptance of this truth and belief in a way of doing something about
it prompted the writing of this book.

For help received, space permits the mention only of those most
closely related to the project, though appreciation is no less real for
the large number of persons who gave understanding support: leaders of professional stature in language arts, teachers in our country
and abroad, colleagues at the University of Denver, and students in
language arts classes.

Gratitude is expressed to Dr. Harold E. Moore, Director of the
School of Education, University of Denver, and Dr. Louis H. Braun,
formerly Administrative Director of the Department of Instruction,
Denver Public Schools (now Superintendent of Schools, Bronxville,
New York), without whose administrative efforts the enterprise
could not have been undertaken.

The teachers whose names appear on the title page gave invalu-
able assistance from the beginning to the end of the project. Believing that talking is a form of communication which must be
learned and that it is learned best in the relationships in which it is
used, they ordered their classroom programs accordingly. From them
came examples of talking which, augmented by contributions from
two other Denver Public School teachers[1] and the author, furnished
the basis for the text.

And what of the children—some three hundred of them, ranging
in age from eight to twelve years—who literally talk their way through
the pages of the book? Here are Carol, Danny, Peter, Annie . . .
with their individual assets and limitations. Their talking was for
fun and the need to share their thoughts and feelings. How surprised they would be to find themselves here!

[1]Alma Mae Greenwood, Park Hill Elementary School and Betty Schnurr, West-
wood Elementary School.

vii

The teachers and children mentioned in this book are all real persons, although they have been given new names in the interest of granting anonymity to schools, classes, teachers, and pupils.

The examples of talking, captured by tape recorder or the stenographer's pencil, have not been polished to perfection but allowed to remain childlike, smoothed only enough to make reading easy and ideas clear. Thus the examples show the kind of talking that may be expected in any classroom and reveal clues for teaching. If read to children, these examples may help tune the ear to correct and incorrect forms, and further the building of standards for clarity and style.

Helping Children in Oral Communication comes as an aid in the total teaching program, not as an extra to be added to an already overcrowded schedule. It will be at home wherever talking is used as communication and becoming refined through the process of honest evaluation and intelligent practice.

May the following pages invite to exploration. And may the exploring be less a matter of reading a book than of entering into companionship with teachers who found happiness and satisfaction in helping children in the art of talking.

ALBERTA MUNKRES

Contents

1

Conversing and Discussing

To give in words,
And get in kind,
Until thoughts glint and gleam,
Can light the mind
And warm the heart.
Conversing—this is it.

To think long thoughts,
To keep the line,
So thought adds to a thought,
Can stir the mind
And stretch the reach.
Discussion—this is it.

CONVERSATION IS THE MOST WIDELY USED OF ALL FORMS OF ORAL COM-
munication and one which does not wait on maturity. Strange it is,
therefore, that so little is done about it in the elementary school. For
this condition two popular opinions may be partly responsible—one,
that a person talks "just naturally"; the other, that conversation is
so vague and unorganized that it cannot be taught. Neither of these
is true. Conversational skills have to be achieved. They are learned,
though often unconsciously, in all the person-to-person relationships
of everyday life. They can be improved by conscious effort.

Conversation is difficult. Launched out in a free exchange of
thoughts with other minds, one never knows the subject on which
he may want to give or receive ideas. Never can he guess at the out-

set which of his treasures he will bring forth for the delight of his friends. Least of all can he know in advance the precise form any of his expressions will take—a question, a statement, an exclamation, a complete sentence, a phrase, a single word. In other words, conversation demands, at its best, a spontaneous and creative flow of ideas in the meeting of minds.

While difficult, conversation is at the same time a delight. It enlivens the dullest situation, releases mirth, invites the birth of new ideas, and builds a sense of oneness with other minds and personalities—goals worthy of the adult as well as the growing child.

Conversation can be *taught*. Mrs. Reed went to her first school, after a university summer course in language arts, determined to make conversation mean something to her pupils. She found twenty-seven fifth graders, mostly of German background, who had not yet freed themselves from the mother tongue of their parents. So frequently did they "go the street up" and "turn the corner round" that, with a generous dash of "ain'ts" added, they were practically unintelligible. These children had made sufficient progress by Christmas time that a teacher substituting for three days reported to Mrs. Reed, "The conversation of these children is delightful, in both form and content."

Conversation can also be *caught*. What the teacher likes and does well the children will most likely enjoy and strive to attain. Does the teacher enjoy meeting other minds and sharing ideas? Does he find pleasure in knowing how to start a conversation, turn it, terminate it? Does he like to throw out leads and pick up clues? Does he reread conversations in favorite books and plays to catch the flavor of the speeches and to become acquainted with the characters who uttered them? If so, he is armed with the best possible equipment for teaching children to converse.

Discussion is like conversation in that it involves a person in a give-and-take situation with other persons; it is unlike it in that its chief purpose is usually the solution of some problem which requires sticking to a point. Its difficulties and delights are much like those which attach to conversation, save often there is opportunity to make preparation for thinking about the problem proposed for discussion, even using notes or outline for guidance.

That learning to participate in discussion is important no one will deny. Indeed, our American way of life has need of persons who can give and receive opinions, separate truth from fallacy, state views clearly and modify them in the light of new facts, come to new understandings as a group and act on the results, testing the value and worth of their decisions.

Differentiation between conversation and discussion is made effectively by Tidyman and Butterfield[1] in a chapter devoted to oral communication. This is done through offering examples as well as by the statement of objectives and procedures.

Helpful, likewise, are the theoretical and practical suggestions in *Language Arts for Today's Children*[2] included in a chapter devoted to various aspects of teaching.

In this book, methods of teaching are built around examples of children engaged in conversing and discussing. The story of how each came to be is told and critical thought about procedures is invited under "Comments and queries."

Conversation and discussion, in these instances, were not taught in isolation but in connection with all aspects of the day's program and related to all other types of language activity. Direct teaching in a separate period was used as freely as needed. Much of the teaching, especially that done in relationship with other classroom activities, took but a few minutes of time. Results, out of proportion to the amount of time invested, were achieved partly because the learning had meaning for the children and partly because the teachers realized they were teaching—they were not just waiting for something to happen.

Realizing the difficulties involved in conversing and discussing, smoothness of talking which is possible in prepared speeches and stories was not expected. Many an error was allowed to pass, temporarily, in the interest of preserving spontaneity and encouraging expression of big ideas as well as choice of new and suitable words. Naturally, the teacher had to decide, in the light of individual and group needs, which problems should be disregarded, for the time being, and which could be handled, at the moment, without creating

[1]Willard F. Tidyman and Marguerite Butterfield, *Teaching the Language Arts* (New York: McGraw-Hill Book Co., 1951), pp. 127-45.

[2]National Council of Teachers of English, Commission on the English Curriculum, *Language Arts for Today's Children* (New York: Appleton-Century-Crofts, 1954), pp. 114-19.

feelings of inadequacy and destroying the tone of the conversation or discussion. Needless to say, children were not interrupted for correction.

Pupils were encouraged to evaluate themselves by listening to recordings which they had helped to make. They were also invited to evaluate and be evaluated by their classmates in situations where constructive opinions might rightly be expected. Always an attempt was made to maintain an atmosphere of congeniality.

No grade standards for conversing and discussing were observed. Teachers started with children where they were and moved from that point to increasing adequacy. The final goal was never reached, but always striven for. Comforting it was to note progress in ability to converse and discuss.

Not alone have ways of helping children learn to converse and discuss been made explicit in the examples which follow and the story of how each came to be; quite as definitely has attention been given to other aspects of the problem—what may be conversed about and discussed with profit, times and places appropriate for each (in school and out), and why one should learn to talk anyway.

No one, not even the teacher whose work is here represented, would follow with another group precisely the procedure presented with a given example. However, anyone can find here suggestions, meanings, insights which are universal in application. In the last analysis, each must teach in his own way because he is the person he is. Nevertheless, each stands to learn from the sincere and productive efforts of his comrades everywhere.

TURTLES, CLAMS, AND OCTOPUS
(Before-school conversation)

Jerry: When I went fishing with a boy, we caught a whole bunch of turtles.

John: Paul on the farm caught a few snappers. He put them in his pocket and went back in the house and had sores all over him. He'd better empty all his pockets.

Bobby: We went to City Park and saw some prehistoric monsters.

Jim: We went to England.

Bobby: England!

John: What did you see?

Jim: A Punch and Judy show that had a dog in it. The dog could do tricks.

Bobby: My dog can do tricks too. He knows how to shake hands. And he can say his prayers.

Stevie: I went to the Pacific Ocean and went down to the sea—uh— and we dug clams.

Richard: I was down on the beach with my cousins in California. Aunt Lou said, "Come on, let's go into the water." Well, something caught my leg and I thought it was an octopus! I ran and I tripped and fell and it was just a little bitty old seaweed.

Jerry: Snapping turtles have real hard shells.

HOW IT CAME TO BE

Miss Williams believes that children learn to converse by conversing, and that part of her job is to develop in children a sense of responsibility in knowing what is appropriate to talk about, when to converse and how to do it well. She realizes that standards evolve from experience and advance progressively from level to level following a general sequence.[3] Believing this to be true, she started not with rules but by declaring a free conversation period. To her surprise, she found that the pupils sat looking at her as if to say, "What do you want us to do?" "What should we talk about?"

Miss Williams suggested the desirability of talking about what one has heard or seen or read, always trying to select items that are interesting to listeners. She stressed the idea that a person can find something to talk about no matter where he lives. All he needs to do is keep his eyes and ears open. Examples of experiences to talk about were then given by members of the class. This was followed by a period in which pupils listed things they might talk about to parents, classmates, and strangers. They were asked not to use single words (trip, pet) but state their ideas so the reader could understand what they had in mind (my trip to the zoo, tricks my dog can do).

Further study brought out such ideas as doing one's part in conversation, not too much and not too little; giving everybody a chance and trying to bring in the person who says nothing; responding to other people rather than merely waiting for a turn.

[3]Ruth G. Strickland, *The Language Arts in the Elementary School* (Boston: D. C. Heath & Co., 1951), pp. 146-50.

Progress was noted at the next period declared free for conversation and the children asked if they might do it again some day.

Miss Williams' goal was to help the children handle conversation well throughout the day, in connection with their classroom activities, at free times before classwork began and at recess if they remained inside, as well as in a period designated for conversation.

To some of the pupils it was a new thought that Miss Williams approved of talking save in response to a raised hand. To most of them, the idea that they were actually learning something in language when they conversed, was a bit startling and not a little intriguing.

Experimentation went forward, somewhat timidly at first, with one eye on the teacher. When it was apparent that nothing was going to happen, the bolder ones became more loquacious, and finally talking was going on so loudly and constantly before and during school hours that confusion resulted.

This was the time to do some evaluating. The teacher asked the children what they thought of the situation and got such answers as:

Stevie: I can't hear a thing.

Jane: He yells all the time.

Jerry: I think you ought to make us stop.

"Maybe you can do something about it," said the teacher. "Suppose we ask ourselves a few questions." Noting the assent of the pupils, she began, "Am I learning how much talking to do when I arrive at school early?" Most of the children knew their answers must be "No." There was no need to poll the class. "Am I learning when to talk and when not to talk during the day?" No answer was needed.

"Perhaps if we set up a few questions to ask ourselves about when and where to talk and how to do it, we might help ourselves," said the teacher. It was agreed and the following questions came from the pupils and were written on the board, later to be transferred to a wall chart. Others were to be added as needed.

1. Is this a time when nobody will be disturbed by my talking?
2. Will I keep myself from doing other things which need to be done, by talking now?

3. Am I listening as well as talking?

4. Am I speaking in a natural tone of voice, not yelling?

"Let's have a conversation period now and see how well we can do it," said the teacher.

When the period came to a close, the teacher and pupils noted situations throughout the day when they would be talking, e.g., social science groups, art class, library period, arithmetic time. Pupils then set themselves the task of keeping in mind the four questions on the chart.

Conversation began to come under control and eventually a happy medium between "no talking" and miscellaneous, idle chatter was reached. An example of a "before-school" conversation (see p. 4), touched off by an article on turtles in a school paper, was caught by the tape recorder.

Judged by the attention of the group members, each had selected something that was of interest to others. All of them could have answered "Yes" to the evaluative question, "Am I learning to think of things to talk about—things that will interest others?" Each one took his turn, although Jerry made use of his second opportunity by continuing what he was saying earlier. Evidently he had not been listening, just waiting. Confusion of thought is betrayed by one long, run-on sentence, and failure to differentiate between fact and belief shows in John's ideas about snappers and sores. One of these would be handled in language period; the other, in science class.

Miss Williams moved from conversation to discussion. After studying how the two are alike and different, she had several of each tape-recorded. Children who had not participated listened to see if they could say which was which. Only three out of the fifteen failed in the identifications. Stated in general terms, the children came out of these experiences saying, "In conversation, you can keep bringing in new ideas and change the subject; in discussion, you must stick to the point because you have a problem to solve."

COMMENTS AND QUERIES

Although Miss Williams believes that children learn to converse through conversing, she does not believe in relying on incidental learning. She believes that much direct teaching must be done both in situations where children are talking and in separate study periods. Her goal in direct teaching is to have the items studied meaningful to the children and recognized by them as related to their needs.

Many opportunities for conversing present themselves through the school day. These are the times when children not only talk but learn to talk better. What are the advantages of having the children identify such situations?

In attempting to find a happy balance between silence and unnecessary and miscellaneous talk through the day, how well did the teacher handle the problem of freedom and control? Were there advantages in helping pupils achieve control for themselves? In what ways would the situation have been different if the teacher had laid down rules to be followed or if the pupils had made rules before they did any experimenting?

What values come to children in bearing complete responsibility for a conversation like "Turtles, Clams, and Octopus"—knowing what to talk about and how to do it satisfactorily? Does this bear any relationship to conversational situations outside the classroom, e.g., a party or club meeting? These children talked not about what they had read in a paper but about their individual, firsthand experiences.

Since conversation is greatly augmented by the number and variety of one's personal experiences, how can children be helped to make the most effective use of the environment in which they live? This includes radio, television, movies, and reading, as well as direct contact with the physical aspects of environment. Are there ways of teaching children to use eyes and ears, as well as other senses, discriminatingly?

The terms "conversation" and "discussion" are often used interchangeably. Is it desirable to differentiate between the two? Note that the pupils in Miss Williams' class, almost without exception, could detect differences as they listened to recordings. Did they hit upon differences that were significant?

"Turtles, Clams, and Octopus" can be read to the children as an effective contrast to the discussion, "Class Flags" (p. 11).

HOW TO ACT AT A PARTY
(Conversation with two dramatizations)

Who wouldn't want to know how to act at a party!

Mr. Baldwin, teacher of grade six, had noticed the quick response of his pupils when this question arose one day. With eagerness the boys and girls had seized upon such ideas as how to avoid being a wallflower; what to do when you can't think of anything to say; how to make new friends.

"Could be," thought Mr. Baldwin, "this is one of their real needs." This impression was strengthened when, a few days later, the discussion came alive in reading and talking about how to make introductions.

"I'll bide my time and watch for an opportunity," thought the teacher. "We'll do something real about this some time." The opportunity came three days later.

HOW THEY CAME TO BE

"In going over the 'Right This Way' column of the *Junior Scholastic* newspaper," Mr. Baldwin said, "I came across the problem of what to do when one is at a party where all, except the host and hostess, are strangers. The answer was to introduce oneself, mingle with other guests, know what to do when you are introduced, say something of interest to the people you meet.

"After much discussion, we decided to pretend. Carol and Bill were chosen as host and hostess; Jane was sent from the room; the rest of the class pretended to be engaged in conversation, games, cards and the like."

(Jane entered and smiled at the group. She then walked over to Carol, the hostess.)

Jane: Hi, Carol!

Carol: Hello.

Jane: It looks like a nice party.

Carol: Yes.

Jane: Am I late?

Carol: No.

(Carol remained seated and Bill, the host, neither rose nor spoke.)

"I broke it up at this point and we discussed what was wrong.

All recognized that the situation was awkward and not comfortable as it should have been. Several mentioned the fact that the host and hostess had failed to do their part in making Carol feel welcome. Some saw that the guests had responsibility too. We studied briefly how to make and acknowledge introductions, as well as how to get the conversation going.

"We decided to try again, choosing three other pupils to be the main characters in the dramatization. John and Mary took their places at the front of the room as host and hostess; Sherry, the guest, left the room; other members of the class became engaged in party activities, as previously."

(Sherry entered the room, smiled and walked over to Mary and John.)

Sherry: Hello, Mary . . . John!

Mary *(jumping up):* O, hello, Sherry! We're so glad you came. Have you met any of the boys and girls?

Sherry: No I haven't, but they seem like a nice bunch.

Mary: Well, come on! We'll go meet some of them.

(Host, hostess and guest go over to two pupils who are seated near the window.)

Mary: Patty and Bob, this is Sherry. She is new in our school.

Bob *(rising):* Hi, Sherry!

Patty: Where do you live?

Sherry: My home is in Buffalo, New York, but we may move to Denver. I certainly hope so because I like it here.

Patty: I hope so, too, for we can have lots of fun together.

Mary: Sherry will be back, but I want to introduce her to some others now.

Patty: Hurry back, Sherry.

Sherry *(smiling):* I will.

Bob: I'm glad I met you.

"At this point, I broke in. We discussed what was good about the second experience. Comments were that everybody felt at ease and it seemed like the real thing.

"I asked if there seemed to be any point in Sherry's saying she liked Denver. The reply came quickly, 'Yes, it made us like her immediately.' Incidentally, Sherry *was* from Buffalo and she *did* move to Denver. It appeared that the pupils really did like her

better because of her remark about their home city, even though
it was made in a 'pretend' situation."

Was dramatization, with conversation an essential part of it, a
happy choice of technique for teaching how to act at a party? Better
than merely discussing the problem? How closely did the classroom
situation approximate a party situation? Note the carry-over from a
pretend to a real situation.

How easy it would have been for the teacher to have stopped with
the first experience, satisfied that it was good enough or the best that
could be expected of children. Failure was turned to success not by
mere repetition nor pressure of any kind, but by teaching—helping
pupils see where they had failed, giving needed instruction, and pro-
viding a second opportunity.

Pupil evaluation was important in this instance, since sensing
rightness and wrongness in a social situation was essential to growth
in learning. The two attempts gave excellent opportunity for learning by contrast. All recognized the second as successful.

"I'll watch for an opportunity," Mr. Baldwin had said to himself. He saw it in a paper though he might have found it in a dozen
other places. Happily, no classroom is without its opportunities, its
moments. Fortunate the teacher with eyes to see and ears to hear!

Children can listen to the two attempts at dramatizing how to act
at a party and see if they know why one is good and the other poor.
They can use them as a help in dramatizing other aspects of social
life.

CLASS FLAGS
(Discussion)

Leader: What shall we do with the flags we've made?
Jimmy: Why couldn't we Scotch-tape them onto the desks and have
 them hang over?
Leader: But you can't put Scotch tape on the desks.
Jimmy: Put anything on.
Leader: Can't put anything on.
Ken: If we had one of them there stands, we could have it settin'
 over at the side of the room, some place, with our flags on it.

Jimmy: But I think everybody would like to have his flag on his desk.

Teacher: Let's find out.

Leader: How many in favor of having a stand with forty flags on it, sitting at the side of the room? [*10 hands*] How many in favor of having your flags on your desks, in some way? [*30 hands*] Well then, we're going to have the flags on our desks, in some way. Now we've got to think of a way to get them there.

Danny: We could take a string and tie them onto the backs of our chairs.

Jimmy: But anyone coming in the door couldn't see the flags.

John: We could have a string across the desk and let the flag hang down over the front of the desk.

Bob: Why couldn't we just lay them on our desks?

Jimmy: But they'd be falling on the floor and you'd be pushing them off.

Teacher: Which do we want?

Leader *(after a vote):* Most of us want to have a string across the desk and have the flag hanging down.

HOW IT CAME TO BE

The boys and girls in grade six were highly individualistic in character. They seemed to have no sense of social solidarity, and hence often engaged in arguments and not infrequently became disciplinary problems.

Mr. Lane felt that neither lecturing nor scolding would produce the desired results. On the contrary, he watched for every possible opportunity to build toward social feeling and group unity.

One of his opportunities came when new encyclopedias arrived. Pages showing colored flags of the nations and various states attracted attention at once. So much talking was done about them that eventually everybody in the room had turned to those pages. If the volume were away from the shelf even briefly, Mr. Lane would hear someone inquiring, "Where is the F book?"

Conversation in small informal groups spilled over into class activities.

Jimmy: Every country has a flag, doesn't it, Mr. Lane?

Teacher: Yes, it does.

Danny: You don't even have to be a country to have a flag. I saw one for Minnesota.

Bob: Mr. Lane, couldn't we draw and color some of those flags?

May: I think it would be nicer if we made our own.

Teacher: What do you mean by "our own"?

May: Oh, our class.

Several: Yes!

Teacher: What would it be like?

Jimmy: Each of us could make one, then we could vote for the one we like best.

Several: Yes!

Pupils then offered ideas as to what might go into a flag which would be suggestive of their room—something about communication which they had been studying (telephone, letters, newspaper) ; something about transportation (airplane, train, rocket ship) ; stars for astronomy experiences; an "S" for their school; a "6" or "VI" for their grade. The colors chosen were blue and gold.

One period was spent in making the flags and voting on the one chosen by the majority to represent all. Another period was spent in making individual copies of the flag. The question then arose as to where the individual flags would be kept and was answered in a group discussion under the leadership of one of its members. (See p. 11.)

Only once did Mr. Lane enter into the discussion and that was when he thought progress would be facilitated by pausing for a vote —an opportunity which he thought would not be recognized by the leader. That the leader learned from the experience is indicated by the fact that he rounded off the discussion by a vote and stated the results to the class.

Inasmuch as speaking had to be done extemporaneously, Mr. Lane thought the talking was clear and as nearly correct as could be expected. He noted that Ken needed to relearn two expressions— "them there" and "settin' "—and made a mental note about caring for them individually. There was a chance that Ken had heard the correct forms as the leader used them. On the other hand, that possibility could not be relied upon.

More work was needed on how to carry on a good discussion. Why not call for an evaluation now?

Patty: We did stick to the point.

Ken: We voted and did what the most of us wanted.

Leader: Jimmy talked every time.

Teacher: What do you mean by "every time"?

Leader: When the kids had ideas. I didn't know how to stop him.

Teacher: You shouldn't have to stop him. He should stop himself.

Mr. Lane recognized the fact that Jimmy needed to understand his habit of disapproving everybody's offering and possible reason for so doing. But that must be done in private and wait upon the proper occasion.

The flags were displayed proudly on the desks where they stayed for days. "Our flag" the children were inclined to say. All seemed to agree when Jim explained to the principal who came to look at them, "We decided to keep them on our desks."

COMMENTS AND QUERIES

To imply that a single group experience like the one described wrought the miracle of a united class is to be unrealistic. It did not. Mr. Lane had to work for months before he began to see results that were more than fleeting. The fact remains, however, that he did achieve results by working steadily, trying always to help the pupils help themselves, to see the results and to like what they saw.

In this case, Mr. Lane accepted a suggestion that came from the class and used student leadership in working it out, in so far as that seemed possible. Two significant words came into the vocabulary of the pupils—"our" and "we."

Jimmy had made something of a nuisance of himself in the discussion period. What are the advantages of helping the boy privately rather than exposing him before the group? In searching for the cause of his behavior, under the guidance of the teacher, Jimmy came to see that the rejection of his proposal at the beginning of the discussion made it hard for him to see others succeed. "I guess I wanted to be just as good as the other kids," was his way of putting it. To see and understand was all that was necessary at the moment, so Mr. Lane thought. Incidentally, his best help had come from Axline's *Play Therapy*.[4]

[4]Virginia M. Axline, *Play Therapy*. Boston: Houghton Mifflin Co., 1947. Chapter 16.

How important is a sense of group unity from the standpoint of personal and social growth? How is it related to mastery of the so-called "school subjects"? Are there advantages to using Mr. Lane's approach over taking charge of the group and stating rules with penalties attached for such types of behavior as argumentativeness and quarrelsomeness?

Listening to the reading of "Class Flags" can give children a feeling of participating in a discussion, where each person does his part—and Jimmy overdoes his. Hearing "Class Flags" and "Turtles, Clams, and Octopus" read in quick succession, helps to differentiate between conversation and discussion.

WHAT SHOULD I DO?
(Discussion)

The boys and girls in Mr. Brown's room keep a question box into which they put questions they would like to have discussed by their classmates. On Friday afternoon the box is opened, the questions removed and read, and a vote taken as to the problem of greatest interest to the whole class. Discussion then proceeds under student leadership, with the teacher standing by for any help that may be needed.

HOW IT CAME TO BE

One Friday afternoon, the following questions were found:

1. A boy is always bothering me. He put a black ink spot on my arm. What should I do about him?

2. The leader of the boys' line usually stops to let the girls come into the room first. Half of the boys get into the girls' line and try to get into the room first—all out of order. Can we do something about this?

3. If you are playing with a boy and another boy comes out and you'd rather play with him, what do you do?

4. My mother always picks company time to scold me for something. How can I tell her how embarrassing it is to be scolded when my friends are around?

5. My grandmother is always buying my clothes and she never picks out anything I like. I don't want to hurt her feelings, but what can I do?

On this particular occasion, question number 5 was selected for consideration and the following discussion ensued.

Leader: What do you have to say about this problem?

Carolyn: She could ask her grandmother not to buy her clothes, in a polite way.

Leader: Are there any more suggestions?

Jean: I think she ought to appreciate all the trouble her grandmother went to to get them, and wear them when her grandmother is around. But she doesn't always have to wear them. I think all she has to do is pretend she likes them, but deep down she doesn't.

Mary: I don't like that idea of pretending.

Janet: Why not?

Mary: Because it's not on the square. Anyway, her grandmother would know she was just pretending.

Jean: Well, then, I think she could ask her grandmother in a nice polite way if she could help buy some of her own clothes.

Rose: She might ask her grandmother if she could try to buy her own clothes and if it worked, her grandmother wouldn't have to worry about it.

Mary: She could—well—she could do things to prove she was—uh—responsible—uh—capable of picking out her own clothes.

Leader: Like what, Mary?

Mary: Well, she could always take care of them and know what to wear—how to match everything.

Carolyn: Maybe she could call her grandmother and suggest some of the things the other mothers buy for their children.

Jack: Let's see, I think she could maybe call . . . us . . . a friend of hers . . . get her friend . . . call a friend of hers and see about it and then it . . . us . . . well . . . ahem . . . . [*laughter*]

Ann: She could have her grandmother call another mother who knows what clothes children should wear.

Leader: Well, that is all the time we have. We hope our ideas have helped the one who asked the question.

COMMENTS AND QUERIES

Mr. Brown believes that his pupils are finding real help for them-selves through the discussion of their personal and social problems. The problems, which at first seemed made-up and artificial, are coming to have the ring of reality to them. Likewise, the discussion grows increasingly genuine.

That these children are able to think about their problem is indicated by the clarity of their statements—all save Jack's. That Jack didn't have an idea, at least not a clear one, might easily have been stated by any member of the group.

The idea of pretending what one did not think or feel was caught by Mary and with the cooperation of the leader explored sufficiently to make everybody conscious of the issues involved.

Mr. Brown remarked about two important words used by Mary—"responsible" and "capable." He brought out the idea that they were just right for the occasion. He suggested, also, that it was better for Mary to hesitate twice and say "uh" while thinking about these new words than to run along quickly and smoothly and use words which were less good or overworked.

Notice that the children built group feeling by talking back and forth, not always to the leader. Mary felt free to challenge Jean's statement and Janet in turn questioned Mary. Jean was influenced sufficiently to change her mind or, at least, to offer another kind of suggestion. Suppose, incidentally, the teacher had been leading the discussion and had challenged Jean with, "That's not nice, is it? Can't you think of something better to say?" How would that have affected group feeling? Freedom of expression?

Mr. Brown believes in student leadership (rotated) in the handling of these questions. Do you think the advantages (i.e., growth in leadership power, feelings of growing up) outweigh the limitations (e.g., lack of experience)?

A study of "What Should I Do?" can assist children in identifying problems of their own on which they need help. It may also lend courage in bringing them into the open and thinking about them honestly with their classmates.

CRACKERS TO EAT
(Conversation after an excursion)

After a class excursion to the Jones Biscuit Company, four boys and girls came into their classroom the next morning laughing and talking about their experience.

Neil: They [the bakers] gave us some nice fresh crackers.

Carol: Right out of the oven!

Donna: Still warm!

All: Yes!

Neil: It's funny how they roll the dough through there.

Carol: They send it through the oven. There are little doors that you look in and see how it is coming along.

Larry: They roll it [the dough] through there and let the prints come down and mark it so it is like crackers. Then they [the bakers] salt 'em and stick 'em in the oven and when they [the crackers] come out . . . .

Carol *(in a loud whisper to Neil):* 'Em! We learned about that just yesterday.

Larry *(continuing):* the girls on each side take long sticks and break them up and we get to eat them.

HOW IT CAME TO BE

John Martin placed his recording machine on a small table near his desk and switched the button that set it going. He was thinking, "Any minute, now, the children will be here and they should be full of talk this morning after the trip to the Jones Biscuit Company yesterday."

Mr. Martin was remembering the interest of the boys and girls in studying about how to converse well—each one do his part, give everybody a chance, follow the conversation and don't merely wait to speak again, try to make everybody in the group comfortable. Yes, the children had thought that interesting; indeed, they had seemed to be making conscious effort to put these ideas into practice.

And how they had seized upon that word "wallflower"! They rolled it over their tongues with satisfaction; even drew pictures of it—a party with everybody in the room playing a game, save one—he, off to one side, alone—a wallflower! They had been entering into conversation so eagerly, each seeming to say, "Catch me being a wallflower!"

But, the teacher reasoned, the periods of conversation in social science and science had been under his guidance—here a question, there a suggestion with, now and then, a word of commendation. But what could these children do, on their own—in a completely unsupervised situation? This he wanted to know. Pondering the question, he had decided to make provision for such an experience and to use the tape recorder to pick up some of the results.

The children were entering the room singly, by pairs and in small groups—by front door and back door. Four boys and girls came in, laughing and conversing about their experiences of yesterday. They lingered near the teacher and his desk and, incidentally, the recording machine, until they had finished expressing the thoughts in their minds.

"Did you take that down?" the children cried as the teacher switched the button. Mr. Martin nodded. "Can we—may we hear it played back?" cried Don. "Later," said Mr. Martin, "all of us will hear it."

Meanwhile, the teacher had noticed as he glanced about the room that the pupils—all 42 of them, 28 boys and 14 girls—had settled into small conversation groups—all, save Danny. Leaning toward Don, he said, "Wouldn't you like to ask Danny into your group? Remember, he was sick yesterday and couldn't go." Speaking to the small group he added, "You will have much to tell him."

"Sure!" answered Don and with a quick turn toward Danny beckoned with a generous wave of the arm as he called, "Come on, Danny!"

Nine o'clock came and went, 9:05, 9:10, 9:15. "They're enjoying it," thought the teacher, "and everyone's doing his part!"

Moving here and there among the small groups the teacher caught phrases—"tasted good," "that big roller," "the baker." He heard not a few words and combinations of words which had been learned incorrectly and were now being used with utter confidence—this here, hisn, can for may, git for get, 'em for them.

Mr. Martin wondered, at first, if he had handled sufficiently well the work dealing with words that needed to be relearned. Had not he and the pupils spent one whole period reading and discussing the matter, and studying the steps to be taken in relearning a word or combination of words? Admit the error, say the correct form several times, say the incorrect and the correct forms so as to note the difference in sound, say the new one alone many times, use it soon and often in talking. Had they not worked to discover the particular words this class and the individuals in it needed to learn? And what a list it was!

Then Mr. Martin became more reassured, remembering Dawson's warning[5] that progress on form is necessarily slow. After all, he thought, it will take a long time to get this job done. And we worked on only three of the words yesterday—'em for them, can for may, hisn for his.

The sound of the tape recorder brought the pupils to attention. "We have something to hear," announced the teacher. "It is a conversation of two girls and two boys—Donna and Carol, Larry and Neil. Listen and see how well you can understand what they say." (See p. 17.)

Jack: I didn't understand all that Larry said.

Teacher: Larry, you and Neil need a word which you do not have. You spoke about rolling the dough "through there." What did you mean?

Larry: Through them things.

Teacher: What are those things like?

Neil: Kind of like rollers.

Teacher: That is exactly what they are—rollers.

Jane: Larry said " em."

Henry: He changed, though.

Teacher: That was good, Larry. You were thinking on your feet, weren't you?

Mr. Martin glanced at his watch (9:30!) then spoke to the class, "Other kinds of work need to be done on our food unit, but first let's listen to the record again. Remember "through the rollers" and "them!"

These boys and girls are ready for more word study, thought the teacher, mentally sorting out a few conspicuous needs as he turned to the recording machine. And remembered, as he released the button, that the children had picked up two of those they had studied the day before.

COMMENTS AND QUERIES

In connection with "Crackers to Eat," the teacher provided the following kinds of experiences on four consecutive days:

Tuesday: Thinking about how to converse

[5]Mildred A. Dawson, *Teaching Language in the Grades* (Yonkers, New York: World Book Company, 1951), pp. 273 ff.

Wednesday: Discovering reasons for learning to converse and spending most of the time thinking about how to escape being a wallflower at a party, the point of interest in the group

Thursday A.M.: Discovering words the children use incorrectly and need to relearn, with a follow-up period for study of individual problems

Thursday P.M.: Visit to the Jones Biscuit Company

Friday A.M.: Experiences recorded, with a look toward more of the type of work done on Thursday morning.

How would the results of this period have differed if Mr. Martin had said one morning, without any preliminary, "Suppose we have a conversation period this morning. You may talk about anything you wish. Wouldn't you like to do some recording so you can hear how well you talk?"

These children were quickly motivated to learn how to converse, but they were slow in relearning incorrect expressions, hence the emphasis indicated. Children, whose home ties have been threatened by a sudden new way of talking, were under no pressure to make changes at once.

As to which words and combinations of words should be attacked, Mr. Martin relied on the needs of his pupils, checked by the suggestions in his language books. He also consulted Pooley's two lists in Dawson's book [6] and found particularly suggestive the forms recommended for omission. This helped him define "good colloquialism," and set some limits in a situation where the needs of the pupils were many and varied. Was it worth while having children talk in small informal groups under their own direction, without a final check by the teacher? Might this conceivably contribute to feelings of responsibility and self-direction in learning? Was the extension of the period, on this occasion, justifiable? Might some other period, on another occasion, be extended at the expense of language activities, thus balancing the time budget?

Many leads for learning form are suggested by this conversation. These and other leads, revealed in a classroom give-and-take, furnish valuable aids for helping children learn to talk clearly, interestingly, and accurately.

---

[6] Dawson, *op. cit.*, p. 277.

2

Storytelling

As showers in springtime
Refresh withered flow'rs, so
Stories like magic
Set children aglow.

And all who behold them,
Know well by their faces,
That rain has been falling
In dry, thirsty places.

STORYTELLING IS MAGIC. IT IS LIKE RUBBING ALADDIN'S LAMP TO MAKE things happen; saying the secret word to waken the sleeping princess; or granting wishes dearest to the heart. In imagination, one goes to lands far away or near, to times that are new or old. With the story-teller go his listeners and stay 'til the tale is told.

Storytellers are made—not born—although often the "making" goes on so early in life at the knee of a storytelling nurse or parent that the art seems natural and unlearned. Fortunately, however, learning can begin at any time where there is a person, child or adult, who believes, who desires, and who is willing to work.

Many helps await the teacher who aspires to become competent in this field—radio and television interpretations; collections of stories which have stood the test of time; classified lists of stories available in any good library; writings on the techniques of story-telling by those who have tried and succeeded.

22

Within easy reach of all is the booklet *Storytelling*[1] with helpful suggestions by a dozen or more writers, among them Madeleine Dixon, Alice Dalgleish, Hughes Mearns, and Helen Orton Fuller. Mildred L. Batchelder, in her list of books for the storyteller, puts the seeker in quick touch with highly selected and very usable resources.

In addition to the books mentioned later in this chapter in connection with the tape recordings, several others, which serve particular purposes, may be cited here.

The well-known and long-loved *How to Tell Stories to Children*[2] speaks helpful words on the necessity of feeling (appreciating) and knowing (not memorizing) the story, and advises telling it "simply, vitally, joyously."

The Art of the Storyteller,[3] written by the renowned English storyteller, Marie Shedlock, suggests artifices by which one endeavors to attract and hold the attention of an audience—pausing for effect; use of mimicry (if one can do it naturally) ; watching the audience; using hands to help express feeling. Types of beginnings which capture the attention of the audience are given and endings which bring the story to a well-rounded conclusion without detracting from the climax, and free the minds and hearts of listeners for appropriating the tale just ended.

Help on choosing words for the building of vivid pictures is one of the most important offerings of Woutrina A. Bone in *Children's Stories and How to Tell Them.*[4]

Telling stories is an art in its own right, not to be confused with the art of reading stories. And since no one can give what he does not possess, becoming a storyteller oneself is the surest guarantee of helping children learn to express their thoughts and feelings through the story. Through this form of communication, a teacher can hope to help children win the kinds of responses from listeners which caused Gretchen to declare, "I just love to tell stories. It feels so good when you finish."

[1]Frances Mayforth (ed.) , *Storytelling*. Washington, D.C.: Association for Childhood Education International, 1942.

[2]Sara Cone Bryant, *How to Tell Stories to Children* (Boston: Houghton Mifflin Co., 1905) , pp. 83-109.

[3]Marie Shedlock, *The Art of the Storyteller* (New York: D. Appleton and Co., 1932) , pp. 31-42.

[4]Woutrina A. Bone, *Children's Stories and How to Tell Them* (New York: Harcourt, Brace and Co., 1924) , pp. 81-103.

Telling stories rightly precedes the writing of stories, leaving the child free from the mechanics of writing (spelling, penmanship, punctuation) while he orients himself in the feel of the story through spontaneous verbal expression. Six stories, as they were created and told by children, are presented in this chapter.

It will be observed that no two teachers made exactly the same approach to storytelling. Some began with characterization, others with form, while others took their start from play with words. All counted on a good background of reading and listening.

In no instance was a "unit" built around storytelling. In a number of cases, however, several consecutive days were devoted to studying and rounding out some aspect of the problem. Time was spent on other language activities before returning to push ahead on the storytelling front.

Thus did work on storytelling continue throughout the year, as did other types of oral communication, and all of them became related at points where they naturally belonged together, each aiding and abetting the other. Furthermore, all were integrated with the total school program.

Each of the six examples as developed in this chapter is important not as a pattern to be followed meticulously, but as an illustration of the way in which one teacher, in one school, with one group of children achieved results. Moreover, many of the detailed methods can be taken out of context and used in other situations, in the building of different designs suited to the needs of specific groups.

SALT AND PEPPER
(Imaginary story)

My story is called "Salt and Pepper" and it is about a little dog.

He got so lonesome one day when he was about three years old that he decided to run away. He thought he had the best chances of surviving if he went to the woods. So he started out and he only had one blanket which was his best one and he wore that. The only other thing he had was his hopes.

When he got to the woods, he started following a path. It came noon and he hadn't found anything he could eat and he didn't know how to hunt very well. Then night fell and he hadn't had anything to eat or drink since early morning. He went and found a little clearing and he went to sleep.

A little after midnight he heard the cracking of a twig and it awakened him. He didn't know what it was. All he saw was four pairs of glowing eyes and all of a sudden they began to move toward him. These eyes were whitish-red-colors, with white background. He later found they were coydogs or half coyote, half dog. They had the—uh—funny—uh—cowerish face of a coyote. But they had—each one in itself had as much courage as a pack of wolves and they—uh— moved in. . . .

HOW IT CAME TO BE

Playing with words is fun. So thought the boys and girls in Mr. Reynolds' room. Small wonder, when the teacher had a flair for words and liked nothing better than the right word in the right place.

Mr. Reynolds was in the habit of using spare moments for new and different ways of thinking about words. He might step to the board, write "democracy" and ask, "What is the opposite word?" Then would follow suggestions, and a discussion of questions posed by the pupils, e.g., "What word is the opposite of 'monarch' which could be used for the leader in a democracy where everybody has his part to play?"

One day the spelling list contained two words missed by many —"accept" and "except." In a spare five minutes (which many a teacher would have thrown away), Mr. Reynolds suggested the two words be dramatized.

"Lois and James, can you do something that will help us understand what the word 'accept' means?" The two pupils rose and walked to the front of the room. Without time for preparation or even checking with each other, they did the following pantomime. James dropped to one knee, lifted his hands pleadingly toward Lois, then put right thumb and forefinger together to form a ring. This he extended toward Lois who, in turn and promptly, put her left third finger through the ring. A burst of hearty laughter indicated that every person in the room knew what was meant and that the word "accept" described it correctly.

"You've done so well," complimented Mr. Reynolds, "that we might have someone show us the meaning of 'except.'" John, when called upon, chose ten classmates. Nine of these he asked to leave the room; the tenth, Bill, remained with him. "All left the room," said John, "except Bill."

This touched off a lively study of words: new and unusual words, e.g., capable, responsible; words needed to express specific thoughts in areas being studied, such as harvest, combine, tractor; overworked words such as awful, lovely, and good.

The teacher suggested the power of words not only to describe a person so that one could see him, but to convey his mood and maybe a suggestion of his purposes and plans.

This proved to be a take-off for storytelling. Mr. Reynolds stepped to the board and wrote the sentence, "A man walked down the street." "Can you see the man?" "No!" came the answer. "Can you see the street?" "No!," again. "Can you see how the man walked?" By this time everybody was saying automatically, what was true, "No."

"Can you make the man a real person who is on his way to do something real?" was Mr. Reynolds' next question. Descriptive words began to flow in without restraint. The children had the idea, but they were overworking it. The process of selection now began. Eventually, the pupils came out with the sentence, "A bent, white-haired man tottered down the street, leaning on his cane and carrying a letter in his free hand." Other examples followed until they felt ready to create stories, choosing the imaginary type.

With little emphasis on form and great stress on characters, the planning and telling went forward. Irwin's story (p. 24) was one of the first and best.

The children spoke with appreciation of "cracking of the twig," "four pairs of glowing eyes," "coydog" and "cowerish."

The teacher suggested that the expression "his hopes" gave a good idea of how Salt and Pepper felt. He spoke further of the fine turn of sentence used by Irwin: "He thought he had the best chances of surviving if he went to the woods. . . . When he got to the woods he started following a path."

In private, the teacher said to Irwin, "How do you do it?" "Oh," answered Irwin, "I just think up a character, then I get him into trouble and see if I can get him out."

COMMENTS AND QUERIES

Of all the possible approaches to storytelling, Mr. Reynolds chose characterization. Notice that Irwin spoke of his experience accordingly, "I think up a character, then get him into trouble and see if I can get him out." He did not say, "A story has an introduction, happenings, climax and conclusion," as might have been the case if story form had been used for the take-off.

Mr. Reynolds has a liking for words and rich resources on which to draw. This need not, however, discourage the person who is less well equipped. Any teacher, however slim his assets, can do something. He can start where he is and move on from there. The kind of help offered by Tidyman and Butterfield[5] is available to all, as are suggestions in language books for children.

Mr. Reynolds' class was ordinary, in the sense that it represented a wide range of abilities in storytelling. Irwin acquitted himself well. But what about the boy or girl at the opposite end of the scale? Did he compare himself unfavorably with Irwin? Did he do nothing because he couldn't do as well? And, one might ask, what about Irwin? Did he judge his success by the less satisfactory productions of his classmates and feel superior?

As a matter of fact, each pupil produced something, and that without pressure or compulsion on the part of the teacher. Furthermore, many a less able pupil, by virtue of teacher acceptance and his own honest efforts to produce, became released enough to enjoy the Irwins and to applaud their more effective efforts. In turn, the Irwin of "Salt and Pepper" did not (and may he never!) seem to consider himself above his peers, far removed though he was, intellectually, from many of them.

Stated in another way, all pupils had the same assignment, as it were, but each produced according to his potentialities. Thus did the teacher achieve in practice what is often but the sounding of a neatly turned phrase, "the individualization of instruction."

One further word about Irwin. His efforts were not limited to storytelling. Many opportunities to perform tasks beyond the reach of others in the class came to him as the so-called "gifted child."

No mention was made, on this occasion, of the "uhs" which punctuated the last two sentences of "Salt and Pepper," since each seemed to cover a pause necessary for an important thought or word which followed. The teacher prized the results above the smooth speaking of commonplaces.

[5]Willard F. Tidyman, and Marguerite Butterfield, *Teaching the Language Arts* (New York: McGraw-Hill Book Co., 1951), pp. 272-85.

The story's conclusion is omitted so that a teacher may let his pupils try to complete it, by working out ways in which Salt and Pepper might have solved the dilemma in which he found himself. Since this is the work of a child, not an adult, the experience should be not too difficult, and the process might prove rewarding.

CATS AND MOUSE
(Imaginary story)

Once there was a mouse named Philip. He didn't like cheese, but he loved to drink the cats' milk. His favorite sport was chasing cats.

Every time the cats would see the mouse, they'd run and hide. Everytime the cats would start drinking their milk, the mouse would go chase them away, and he'd drink all the milk.

The cats were not getting enough to eat, and they kept getting thinner and thinner. And the mouse kept getting bigger and bigger. The cats got so thin that they vanished. And the mouse got so big he burst. And that's the end of the cats and the mouse.

HOW IT CAME TO BE

Miss Mead is a superior storyteller and uses every possible occasion for sharing with her pupils some tale—imagined, built around her personal experiences or discovered in a book. She believes with Ruth Sawyer[6] in filling the listening years so that the years ahead may never run dry. As a result, Miss Mead's pupils have story sense and, on the slightest provocation, turn out stories for the edification and delight of their classmates, not to mention the pleasure derived for themselves.

On this particular morning, the children, because of their interest in the Paul Bunyan stories, suggested they try making tall tales of their own. About what or whom? Many were the characters named —toad, dog, hippopotamus, fish, grasshopper, giant, horse, tiger, whale. . . .

What was going to happen to these characters? That required thought. Finally, suggestions began to come.

Fred: I'm going to make my dog climb a tree.

[6]Ruth Sawyer, *The Way of the Storyteller* (New York: The Viking Press, 1942), p. 18.

Henry: I'll put my dog in a barrel and have him saved from the flood in that way.

Judy: My rabbit is going to be little and he is going to get lost.

Patty: A whale could go walking at the bottom of the sea. She could have starfish for earrings.

How to get characters out of trouble was the next problem discussed. Examples were given from the Paul Bunyan stories.

May: The fox that was catching chickens got out of trouble by hiding in Paul Bunyan's beard.

Danny: Babe the Blue Ox got scared at an automobile. He leaped over a two-story building and headed for the open country.

Peter: When Babe the Blue Ox was thirsty, he drank the river dry.

These children sensed story form but were unaccustomed to thinking of the terms—beginning, happenings, climax and conclusion. The teacher explained them briefly and said finally, "The big thing you will have to learn is how to begin, move ahead, make the point, and stop."

After working on their tall tales at odd moments, the pupils were given a period in which to round out their ideas. They worked, some at the storytelling table, some at their own desks, some conferring with the teacher. Some made notes; others sat without books, paper, or pencil, looking dreamily out of the window.

The language period on the following day was declared "Story Hour." The children were not only to tell their stories but, at their own request, to record them on tape. "In that way we can keep them," they declared.

Peter's carefully worked out tale (p. 28) pleased the group and elicited much spontaneous conversation.

The recorded evaluation showed that Lois, at any rate, had recognized story form when she said, "Peter planned his story good. All the parts were there." Freedom from pauses and unnecessary connectives was expressed by John in the words, "He didn't have any time when he didn't say anything." Sense of the dramatic prompted David to add, "I think Peter could clap his hands or something when he tells about the mouse getting so big he burst."

Some of the other tall tales told were "How the Hippopotamus Lake Came to Be"; "Green Gooey Goblins"; "A Chinese Fish Named

Wang See"; "The Case of a Strange Grasshopper"; "The Little Weiner Dog"; and "Contrary Goat." All were recorded and played back to the children on the following day.

Annie: Are we going to keep them?

Teacher: Yes, we can keep this tape.

Danny: I wish we could read them.

Teacher: I could take them off and type them.

Several *(eagerly):* Could you?

Fred: Then we could have a book of them.

Patty: We could put it in the library too.

Miss Mead set herself the task of transcribing the stories and stapling them into book form. When the book appeared on the storytelling table, it bore the title, "Telling Tall Tales" and was decorated with the head and very long neck of a giraffe. Squeals of delight greeted its appearance and eager voices called, "Me next!" "Me too!" "Me, me, me!"

The children had fun telling their stories to other groups in the building. Through questions asked by the listeners and comments made by the teachers, many leads for learning were discovered.

Incidentally, one year later, the children still cherish their book of tall tales, and the new group of pupils who have come to Miss Mead are already asking, "When are *we* going to tell tall tales?"

COMMENTS AND QUERIES

Miss Mead does not consider herself a "born" storyteller. She has made herself master of the art by much practice and the help of not a few artists, chief of whom is Ruth Sawyer. Let her success help in removing barriers to storytelling erected in the mind of many a teacher who considers herself not to the manner born! Let this achievement herald the reward of honest effort and invite to the adventure which is storytelling.

Miss Mead offers the following suggestions—not rules—which she kept in mind and used with her pupils as needed when writing imaginary stories.

1. You must have characters to make a story. Who or what are they going to be? Not too many!

2. Your characters must have things happen to them—just enough and not too many.

3. When your characters get into trouble, you must think how to get them out. Whatever you do with them must seem to be right and not silly, though it may be unusual.

4. You will want to remember story form—happenings, climax, beginning and ending.

5. Run through your story once in your mind and you may be ready to tell it.

"The book," as it was called, made tangible the oral efforts of the children and preserved them for future use. It was of definite help in stimulating reading, especially among the less able pupils. Here the recorded evaluations served to encourage discriminating reading, since they suggested weaknesses as well as strong points. Notice the long-range appeal of this book to the children who made it and the motivation it induced in the class that followed.

Sharing the created tall tales with younger children in the building gave dignity to the enterprise, brought pleasure to the listeners and added skills to the tellers. Being evaluated by new audiences gave the tellers increasing insight about the success of their efforts. Discouraged at first by a negative remark or two ("they nudged each other and giggled"), the storytellers learned quickly to overcome their weaknesses in succeeding performances.

"Cats and Mouse" should be compared with "Annie's Icicle" (p. 92) and "Contrary Goat" (p. 89), as a means of noting different ways in which storytellers achieve humor. Various approaches to creative work can also be identified with profit—the spontaneous versus the more carefully planned procedure.

MAMMOTH HUNTERS[7]
(Story read and told)

Beartooth and Swiftboy were going through the groves of the trees and they never found anything and they still went through the groves and they came to the last grove and they still never found anything. Then they went into the wooded valley and they saw a— uh—beast in the bushes where the yellowish-gray dust had—uh— settled up and then Beartooth—uh—Swiftboy said that—uh—Swiftboy said, "Beartooth, you stay up there and watch while I go back to

[7]Nila Banton Smith and Stephen F. Bayne, *On the Long Road.* New York: Silver Burdett Company, 1940.

camp and get the other men." So he started running back at a jag
—jog trout and—uh—then he sat down to rest a while. . . .

HOW IT CAME TO BE

Special interest in stories found in school readers precipitated the
following conversation in Miss Blake's fourth grade.

Mary: I know "Aladdin's Lamp."

Joe: Last year I read a story about a policeman helping some ducks
cross the street.

Mae: I told a story in Campfire last week.

Teacher *(to the class):* Do you know different kinds of stories?

Mark: I know a lot of true-or-might-be-true stories. Bambi is one.

Harriett: Fairy tales are fun. I know they're not true, but I like
to hear about kings and queens and princesses and all that.

Learning to tell a story seemed the next natural step and Miss
Blake thought the experience story might well be the first kind to try.

It happened that this group was studying "Early Man" in social
science. They had made a trip to the museum to familiarize themselves with life as it was lived in the long ago. In small groups,
they were talking about what they had seen when Miss Blake suggested they imagine they were living in that time and make stories
of their experiences. Enthusiasm died instantly. They didn't know
how, they declared. The group began to fall apart, and became contentious.

"I am busy with another group," said Miss Blake. "Why don't you
take paper and pencil and tell me what the trouble is and how you
feel about it." Notations on the papers were revealing:

Jane: I don't know what an experience is.

Jack: I don't know how to make a story.

Mary: I don't know what to tell.

Gretchen: I don't like stories anyway. [Compare this remark with
Gretchen's later attitude. See page 23.]

Miss Blake began to see that she had expected too much of the
group and that a great deal of work must be done before these children could feel adequate in creating and telling experience stories.
Because antagonistic feelings had been built around this type of
story, the teacher let the matter drop, temporarily, and turned to
stories which the children could read and tell.

In this connection, the following suggestions as to how to tell a story which had been read were developed:

1. Read the story carefully.

2. Think how to make a good, clear beginning with only a few complete sentences. Try to use sentences which will make people stop and listen.

3. Think about the right order of the happenings. Write them down, if that will help.

4. Put a star, perhaps, beside the climax of the story. That will show how important it is.

5. Think about the ending and a few sentences needed to bring the story to a close.

6. Study the whole story but do not write it word for word or memorize it.

7. Lay the paper aside, if it has been used, and go through the story without help.

Carol was the first to tell a story she had read. She chose "Three Billy Goats Gruff" which she had practiced in the storytelling club. This she told without hesitation but with little characterization, seeming unable to alter her dainty voice and precise manner of speaking. The children helped her by giving interpretations of the three goats and the troll. She asked to try again, which she did a week later, showing great improvement in making the characters come alive. Roy expressed the feeling of the class when he said, "She made the characters act with her voice."

Carol took her story to first graders in the building and, as reported back to her teacher, "Not one child wiggled, while she spoke."

About that time, "Mammoth Hunters" was studied in connection with reading and, much to the surprise and delight of the teacher, Ronnie offered to tell it to the class.

Ronnie, slightly undersized and anemic looking, had come to Miss Blake with the reputation of being a silent member of the group and one who caused trouble by slipping away at recess although not arriving home until the proper hour in the afternoon. Ronnie! Offering to tell a story!

The experience, although entered into with willingness, was a dismal failure judged by all standards of storytelling. Ronnie cleared his throat so much no one could tell what he was trying to say.

Miss Blake, seeing how discouraged Ronnie was, spoke to him in private. "You can learn to tell a story," she said. "Many people, even grownups, clear their throats when they are scared."

A few days later, when Miss Blake was using the recording machine to pick up stories the children were telling, Ronnie asked if he might tell one. He chose the story attempted earlier and recorded it. (See p. 31.)

When the story was played back, Ronnie was able to make his own evaluation. Said he, "I kept saying the same thing over and over . . . put in some words where they weren't supposed to be . . . made all the characters talk, but not right." He then hung his head as he said, "Just about everything was wrong." Then suddenly he lifted his head, smiled at Miss Blake and said, "But I didn't clear my throat."

This was the beginning of better times. Ronnie joined the storytelling club. He read many, many stories. He told short stories, then longer ones, often recording them and listening to them played back. Ronnie possessed sufficient critical power to keep his efforts from being mere repetition of earlier attempts. He also carried with him all the motivation needed to become a better storyteller.

What Miss Blake suspected at the start and later knew to be true, was that Ronnie did not want to be silent; he was simply scared in school. Only once during the year did he slip away at recess and that was on the day a supply teacher was in charge of the group. Understanding the boy's need for security, Miss Blake overlooked this lapse when Ronnie settled happily into his new-for-this-year pattern, the following day.

COMMENTS AND QUERIES

Miss Blake turned failure into success by dropping what she had undertaken and starting at another point. Was this an admission of weakness on her part and a triumph for an I-can't-do-it attitude on the part of the children? Or was it a matter of sensing that the long way round was the short way to success? Eventually, Gretchen was to be the one to bring the class and teacher back to the main line, as it were. But more of that later.

What was there about telling stories that made Ronnie begin to feel adequate? Maybe it wasn't anything about storytelling, as such; rather something about Miss Blake and the way she handled the matter. Maybe it was the combination of children in the class or those who occupied the table at which he sat. Maybe, to make another guess, Ronnie was growing up a bit and ripe for this opportunity. Perhaps there had been a resolution of some difficulty in the home. More than likely it was a combination of many and sundry experiences.

Suppose Miss Blake had accepted as final the pattern which Ronnie had developed in earlier grades. Suppose she had labeled him a "nonreader" and threatened punishment for truancy. Or suppose she had reserved the fun of storytelling for those who had finished "all their work," including exercises connected with reading. Might she not only have confirmed and made more rigid a pattern already defined? As it was, Ronnie was accepted by the teacher as a worthy individual, and found himself wanting to learn and sufficiently released emotionally to accept the help that was available. A new pattern started growing with no reference ever having been made to the old type of reaction.

Storytelling proved to be the kind of leading-on experience which helped Ronnie learn not only to tell stories but to read (something he had done poorly up to this time) and to participate in other classroom experiences. Best of all, it was an indirect way of helping him to overcome an attitude of fear and to find school a place where he liked to be.

Children who are failing or struggling to succeed will most likely find themselves reflected in Ronnie's "Mammoth Hunters" (p. 31). "Last Match, told months later, shows what can be achieved by an intelligent boy when freed from his fears, and characterized by a will to work.

LAST MATCH[8]
(Story read and told)

This is the story of how the little old lady saved her last match. One morning she was having breakfast and she happened to look in her match box and there was only one match left. So she

[8]Eleanor M. Johnson, and L. B. Jacobs (eds.), *Treasury of Literature*. Read-text series. Grade 3: *Treat Shop;* Grade 4: *Magic Carpet;* Grade 5: *Enchanted Isles;* Grade 6: *Adventure Lands.* Columbus, Ohio: Charles E. Merrill, 1954. ("The Last Match" is from the volume *Magic Carpet*.)

washed and dried the dishes and said to herself, "Tomorrow is market day and I have to save that match if I want to read tonight." So she washed and dried the dishes and set up the ironing board on the backs of the chairs and went to get a soap box to fit the ironing board to stand on.

Then she went out and put the match box on the mantel so it would be safe—the match wouldn't get broken or anything like that. Then she went out and did a few pieces of ironing. After a little bit she stopped and wondered, "Oh, dear, what . . . uh . . . what if the match would get broken."

And she went out and got a piece of cotton and wrapped it, then put it back on the mantel. Then she went out and did a few more pieces of ironing. And she worried about the match. What if it would get damp and she couldn't read that night?

So she went out and got a tin can to put it in and put it back on the mantel. After a little bit she didn't do any ironing at all— 'cause . . . 'cause . . . that she was afraid that the match might not strike that night and she couldn't read. So then she sat down and put a wet towel around her head and said, "What if I just strike it now, then I can do my ironing and finish."

She went out and got the match and unwrapped the cotton from it and took it out of the tin can and struck it on the mantel. The first time it didn't strike and the second time it struck and went into flames. Then after a little bit she went out and did her ironing and finished it.

She started her weekly reading and it was getting dark so she trimmed the wick and started to light the lamp and she couldn't light it 'cause she had used the match. She said she should think before she did it. After a little bit she thought, "Why couldn't I just get a light from the stove and put it on the wick. Then I can have my light for reading." So she got pieces of paper and twisted them and got a light from the stove and lit the lamp and she got to read that night. She said, "Well, I am not . . . I am so . . . I am pretty clever after all."

HOW IT CAME TO BE

"A story is different from just talking," said Miss Blake to her class. "It has form." "Form?" asked the children. "Yes," answered the teacher, "and that means a beginning, some happenings, a climax and an ending." Whereupon, she explained each. Climax—the nub of the story to be held back until just the right moment; happenings —which lead up to the climax (not too many, not too few, just enough and in the right order); beginning—telling who, when, where; end—which comes soon, very soon, after the climax.

The following day the children found stories in their readers and had fun talking about the beginnings and endings, finding the climax in each story and identifying the happenings. They seemed to enjoy using the new word "climax" and old words with new meanings, "beginning," "happenings," "ending."

About that time *Treasury of Literature* was bought by the school and forty copies of *Magic Carpet* were placed in Miss Blake's room.

So great was the excitement at the prospect of new books so attractive to the eye, that Miss Blake took the period ordinarily used for sharing to introduce the book. She did this by reading a few of the titles, displaying some of the pictures and suggesting that anyone might look at a copy in his free time.

The book was picked up by nearly everybody in the class at one time or another, and about half of the class of forty read continuously. Most, though not all of them, were the better readers.

Ronnie (p. 35) not only read, but asked if he might tell one of the stories to the class. He told the story without having to go back and correct himself, but still included many "uhs" and "ahs," and looked out of the window rather than at the class. He did hold the children's interest to the end, however.

The children now began reading to each other from *Magic Carpet* and telling what they had read. In spare moments, they worked by pairs in far corners of the room and out in the hall. In this way, each child in the room became a part of the story program.

Miss Blake thought this a good time for the children to be helped on the problem of how to tell a story. Accordingly, an entire language period was spent learning about some of the artifices of the storyteller—making characters talk, imitating characters, looking at the audience.

Three months passed and Ronnie's interest continued. He had read and told many stories, recording a number of them and listening to hear how they sounded when played back. At last he surprised his teacher and classmates and pleased himself with the long and well-handled story given on page 35.

Ronnie's gain was apparent to his classmates, as evidenced by hearty applause when he finished. Significantly he had improved in all school subjects, including reading. Imagine Miss Blake's delight when, needing to leave the room to answer an important call, the children asked if Ronnie might read to them while she was away.

COMMENTS AND QUERIES

Miss Blake's use of the tape recorder as a means of self-evaluation is worthy of note. Story by story, Ronnie recorded, heard how he sounded, and improved steadily. So firmly does Miss Blake believe in this technique that she keeps her machine in readiness at all times.

Ronnie's growth was not magic, save in the sense that all growth is something of a miracle. It came about gradually as a result of of activities and relationships which stretched over a three-month period of time—activities which included, along with storytelling, dramatization, reporting, conversation and discussion, as well as all other aspects of the day's program.

One might well ask, however, whether all of the other thirty-nine children grew in storytelling power as this boy did. More than "Yes" or "No" is required to answer this question. Some children were abler than he at the beginning, hence showed less change. Some had handicaps unlike his, for example, Gretchen in a new school and struggling with a bilingual background (p. 42). The types of progress were therefore different. Some were less able to evaluate themselves and moved more slowly. Some, who showed little initiative, though as able as Ronnie, moved more slowly than he did. Accounts could be written about each child in the room and no two would be alike. Suffice it to say that in that room there was an air of great excitement about storytelling and that no child lost opportunity or attention because of Ronnie's experiences.

Ronnie was never conscious of being a "problem" boy in Miss Blake's room, nor did the other children think of him as an object of special attention. Classmates did, however, become aware of his "growingness" and, without being conscious of all they were doing for him, accorded him a valued place in their group. Ronnie was no longer out; he was in. And comfortable was the feeling of warmth and friendliness!

"Last Match" (p. 35) and "Mammoth Hunters" (p. 31) should be read consecutively in order to understand how tremendous was the growth made by Ronnie. Shared with children, such an experience might leave the impression, "If Ronnie could do it, so can I."

EXCITING EXPERIENCE
(Experience story)

When I was five or six years old we lived in the country and I was in the kitchen once helping my mother with the dishes. I dropped one of her good ones and broke it. She got mad at me and told me to go out and get the eggs.

So I went out and it was dark in the henhouse and I reached in and felt something cold in the nest. I didn't know what it was so I went back and said, "Mamma, can I have a flashlight? There's something in the nest." She said, "Oh, it's probably an old hen." So she gave me a flashlight and I went back out and shined it in the nest. And there was a black snake coiled up in the nest, swallowing an egg.

I ran out of the chicken house and started jumping up and down screaming, "Daddy, daddy!" And he came out there and killed it and said it would have bit me if it hadn't just swallowed the egg.

HOW IT CAME TO BE

After noting three kinds of stories suitable for telling—those read from books, those made from one's own experiences and heard about other people, and those imagined—the pupils in Mr. Palmer's class decided to work on the second, namely, experience stories.

As a help in this undertaking, one period was spent studying how to prepare an experience story. The following suggestions emerged:

1. Get an idea first.

2. Think of the point of the story—the climax—and plan to hold it back until you are ready to let your listeners hear it.

3. Think of the happenings that lead up to the climax and get them in the right order.

4. Decide on a good beginning that will make people stop and listen, but one which does not give away the climax.

5. Start telling your story and move, step by step, to the climax.

6. Stop after that with a sentence or two for a good ending.

It was decided in a planning period that the children would work in small groups to choose firsthand experiences which might be put into story form. They were then to prepare their stories, individually, using the six points studied, before meeting again to share the results with each other.

The teacher then suggested that each person would probably do his best if he were working with classmates he especially enjoyed. Would they like to write on a slip of paper first, second, and third choices? He would look at all the slips and by tomorrow be able to name the groups. This suggestion was accepted readily and in a few minutes the slips were ready to hand to the teacher, some of them folded once, twice, three times, as if the ballot were most secret.

A study of the choices revealed what Mr. Palmer suspected, namely, that some children were very much alone—receiving not a single vote; others were chosen an inordinate number of times. In several instances, mutuality of choices existed; in others, there was complete mismatching of choices.

Mr. Palmer placed Henry (no votes) in a group with John (his second choice) who was a good leader and could be counted on not to talk all the time and to bring out each member of the group. Jane (an able student), who was inclined to work always with her first and second choices, was placed in a group of which her third choice was a member. Mark, who felt very insecure and inadequate, and was new in the school, was placed with Joe (his first choice) who lived in his neighborhood and came to school by the same route, and with Ned (not chosen by Mark) who was a good friend of Joe.

In the end, there were five groups with eight pupils in each. Each pupil had one of his choices honored.

Without discussion, Mr. Palmer read the names of pupils in the five groups and indicated places where desks could be pulled into circles. The pupils were accustomed to working in small groups, hence the choosing of a leader was considered more or less routine. It was understood that the job of the leader was to give everybody a chance to name some experience he had had or heard about which might make a good story, for example, swimming at the Y, riding a horse in camp, training a pet to do tricks, losing carfare.

Mr. Palmer circulated among the groups with a word here and there, as needed or asked for. He lingered at the fourth group, listening to the conversation.

Leader: But I don't think that is a good idea.

James: But that's what I want to tell. It really happened.

Leader: But I said it wasn't any good.

Teacher: Just a minute, please. What did we say the job of the leader was?

Ned: Keep things going.

James: To let us say what we wanted to make into a story.

Leader: But it wasn't any good.

Teacher: Was the leader to tell how good it was?

Leader: Well, No!

The next day was spent thinking about the experiences and making them into stories to tell in the small groups when they reassembled a few days later.

That was an occasion to be remembered. Enthusiasm ran high. Mr. Palmer could see that participation was prompt and eager. At the close, he called for reports by the leaders and found that four or five in each group had told stories.

The pupils asked if they might hear some of the stories told in groups other than their own. After some discussion, it was decided that each group choose its best one which would then be told to the whole class. From group five came Henry's story (p. 39).

The children reacted to the story with many pretended shivers. They were quick to note that Henry had made them see, hear, and feel what he was talking about. It was, they declared "a good story."

Mr. Palmer's use of sociometric techniques for grouping served him well. Later sociograms compared with the one made on this occasion showed definite gain in socializing with no one left out completely.

The sociogram is not difficult to plot. Detailed help can be found in any number of resources, for example, *How to Construct a Sociogram.*[9] The sociogram represents a graphic way of handling choices made by the children and gives a visual picture of the social

[9]Horace Mann–Lincoln Institute of School Experimentation, *How to Construct a Sociogram* (New York: Bureau of Publications, Teachers College, Columbia University, 1947), pp. 1-23.

aspirations of the children and the degree to which their aspirations are reciprocated. The sociogram makes comparatively easy the formation of groups to help assimilate those chosen by no one, to enlarge a small group which may have become closed and complacent, to call into use the leadership of much-sought children.

Small-group work also had its rewards, not the least of which was indication of growth in leadership ability. Working in small groups created a sense of confidence which would probably not have been possible if sharing had been done, from the first, with the whole class.

The response in creating and telling experience stories was prompt and without interference of any kind. This might be compared with the experiences of another group (p. 31), where a false start was made and a detour became necessary, with a considerable lapse of time before the original purpose was achieved. In the end, however, each group learned to create and tell stories out of their own experiences and had fun in the process.

"Exciting Experience" can help children identify experiences of their own which can be told as stories and communicate the idea that insignificant happenings can be turned into something exciting.

CHRISTMAS IN GERMANY
(Experience story)

Two years ago when I was in Germany and it was Christmas, I wanted a dog and a cat so my grandmother told me to get out of the house. I didn't want to so she pushed me out of the house. And I started to cry so she shut the door on me.

We had an attic and I went up there. I had a little doll up there and I brought it down and played dolls. Then mamma said, "Come in and go to bed."

So I laid down for a while and then I got suspicious. I got up and there was one of my old shoes full of candy and stuff and I put it on [*laughter*] and there was a whole mess of candy in there and I got candy all over my feet [*laughter, again*].

When I got out in the living room there was this big doll at the bottom of the Christmas tree and it was setting on the floor. When I went into the living room, I got scared because I thought it was some real person. Then I went close to it with a big stick and said,

"Is you alive?" I acted real funny 'cause I didn't know it was a doll so I picked it up by one arm and then I dropped it and then I picked it up and took it to my mamma. My mamma said, "What did you get for Christmas?" And I said, "What?" I didn't know that was a doll for Christmas. So she said, "Why don't you take it to bed?"

When I fell asleep zat night, my mother took the doll out of the bedroom.

The next morning I wanted the doll. So I sorta fell out of the bed . . . looked under . . . no doll! I went out to the Christmas tree. I thought maybe my mother had put the doll back up. I didn't see the doll. I looked all around the Christmas tree. Finally, I found the doll wrapped in a package in the back of the Christmas tree.

HOW IT CAME TO BE

Miss Blake held to the idea that her children could learn to create and tell experience stories. But how? She had talked with them and offered help, but nothing happened. The children's sharings in "Telling Time" were still long, rambling recitals of incidents, completely without form. She had tried asking the children to make stories of experiences they might have had in the days of the cave man (p. 32), but the result was confusion accompanied by negative feelings.

Then it was that Miss Blake remembered an idea which had come to her in her university preparation for teaching, "Your pupils will tend to like what you like and enjoy learning what you have mastered—science, poetry, art, storytelling. . . ." Close on the heels of that memory came another and from the same source, "Children want to know what adulthood is like. This they can begin to understand by hearing stories about the experiences of grownups." A third memory followed, "Children enjoy hearing what grownups were like as children. Assurance comes to them in knowing that a child, sometimes foolish and often blundering, can grow into the kind of self-assured person now standing before them."

Looking straight at herself, Miss Blake had to admit that she had never told an experience story to this group or any other. She had not until recently even realized there was such a thing as using the story form for casual experiences about which she talked. She had done as the children were doing—told incidents in any form or order in which they came to mind at the moment.

Sitting at her desk, long after the last child had gone home, Miss Blake laughed aloud as she remembered an experience she once had in visiting a first grade. A charming boy, hair titian red, eyes sparkling blue, came down the aisle swinging his body gently and took his place before the group. He was to play teacher for a few moments and do anything he wished with the class. He chose to carry on a quick drill in number combinations. All went well until, inflated by success, he tossed out a problem far beyond the ability of first graders, including himself. When no answer came, a silence settled over the room and a veil seemed to drop over the face of the would-be teacher. "Do you know the answer, Kenny?" asked the teacher quietly. Kenny's answer was brisk and full of assurance, "Oh, I don't have to know. I am just the teacher. I make them do it."

Yes, that was it, thought Miss Blake. She was trying to make children do something which she, herself, had never mastered.

With a quick ordering of books and papers on her desk—one set went into her briefcase—she reached for hat and coat and was off to the library.

The Way of the Storyteller[10] was first on her list. She became so engrossed in reading it that she looked no further that night. She went home with the strong impression that learning to tell stories required work, part of which consisted in building a background of personal experiences.

Exploring further, she found in Rasmussen's *Speech Methods in the Elementary School*[11] a few good rules to follow and noted that she would want to return to this, later, for help on conversation, discussion, talks, and creative dramatics. A number of books on storytelling in Rasmussen's bibliography would be examined later as time permitted.

When several books had been consulted, Miss Blake came to the conclusion there was little help on the experience story, as such. However, a vast amount, applicable to various types of stories, was at her disposal.

Miss Blake's first experience story, told to the children, had to do

[10]Sawyer, *op. cit.*, especially pp. 81-89.

[11]Carrie Rasmussen, *Speech Methods in the Elementary School* (New York: The Ronald Press Co., 1949), p. 115.

with her vacation trip to New York City at Christmastime.

In Grand Central Station she sought a little clearing in the crowd, rested her suitcase beside her and stared at the vast and moving throng. Thus she stood for a few moments, only to find when she started for the taxi that her suitcase was gone.

"Gone!" cried the children. "Yes, gone!" answered the teacher. "But listen!"

From there on suspense grew as Miss Blake told of hunting, with the help of a policeman, in that enormous crowd and—climax —finding the suitcase standing all by itself on the platform near an outgoing train. Sighs of relief were followed by speculations as to how the bag got there and what had happened to it between then and the time it had left Miss Blake's side.

Many other teacher-experience stories followed, but with no label attached to say, "This is an experience story."

Children were still telling stories they had read, and liking it. They were having fun using some of the tricks of the storyteller's trade, such as making characters talk, pausing briefly before giving away some important or secret idea. They had become conscious of picture-building words, for example, fluttering, scrunch, dazzling. They had read to the class paragraphs from library books which made the listeners see, hear, smell, taste or feel something, in imagination. They had also found particular interest in story form—introduction, happenings, climax, end. Still no experience stories!

Then it happened! Gretchen, of all people, away from Germany less than two years and still practically a stranger in the class, was saying, "Teacher, I could tell about my Christmas doll." And tell about it she did. (See p. 42.)

At first her voice was so low that Carl called out, "Speak up, can't ya!" Somebody wanted to hear her! Everybody was looking at her! Gretchen lifted her head and began to speak to the last person in the back of the room. She looked around, as if she were saying to each one, "I'm talking to you." She began to be released, changed her voice at appropriate points, made her characters talk, laughed with the other children. Gretchen had surprised herself into telling an experience story and the children recognized it as such. "She made a story," cried Carl. "Yes, a story!" echoed the other children.

Miss Blake let the errors pass, not wanting to dim the glory of this moment. At another time, in another setting, Gretchen and other members of the class could tackle the problem of relearning words that had been learned incorrectly, for example, laid for lay, setting for sitting.

Gretchen seemed to gain admittance to the group through this experience. She joined the storytelling club and participated in other activities of the classroom. When she went to another school a few months later, she telephoned Miss Blake to say, "I want to come back to zat school."

Others followed Gretchen's lead and began planning experience stories. Requests for help led to the development of suggestions similar to those on page 39.

The pupils worked mostly in small groups and were helpful to each other in discovering the kinds of experiences that make good stories. They were surprised to learn that a simple, everyday experience could be made into a good story. They need not wait for something unusual to happen nor for an excursion to furnish the necessary material.

About this time they began telling stories to Mother and Father and reported many a happy occasion at the dinner table and in the evening before bedtime.

Miss Blake felt that the goal she had set six weeks earlier and had hoped to achieve promptly had now been reached. Her children could create and tell experience stories.

COMMENTS AND QUERIES

Although weeks passed while Miss Blake was reaching her goal, she and her pupils engaged in many other language activities in the meanwhile. They gave thought to conversation and discussion, worked out a spontaneous dramatization, learned new things about reporting and making speeches. Naturally, other activities of the school day were carried on as usual.

Did the teacher do well to give the children time to grow into creative story making and telling? How did she and the children profit by detouring, then coming back to the main road? Suppose she had taken the attitude at the beginning, "We'll stay with stories and cave men until something does happen?"

Did the teacher do right in overlooking, temporarily, the errors in English? Were there other values more important at the moment? How might the situation have been changed if she had required written exercises immediately after the story, to correct the errors?

Gretchen's mother uses "zat." Can Gretchen be helped to say "that" without feeling estranged from her mother? She shows no emotional response when attempting to make the change. Miss Blake interprets this as meaning, "No danger here!"

"Christmas in Germany" may suggest features of Christmas in our country which could be used in making good stories. It may also help children to identify appreciatively with those in their group who might in any way be considered "different."

3

Reporting and Making Speeches

How dull it can be,
The report that is read
Of words not one's own,
Of thoughts not quite clear;
Dull both to the reader
And hearer, as well;
Encouragement to
The wand'ring of minds.

How bright it can be,
The report that is shared
Of words that have worth,
Of ideas grasped;
Bright both to the speaker
And learner, as well;
An instrument in
The meeting of minds.

REPORTING AND MAKING SPEECHES ARE THE BANE OF MANY A TEACHER'S life—and the pupil's, too. Still they go on, drone after drone, the speaker lost in his own verbiage or that of some book; the listeners, teacher included, sunk into a kind of protective numbness.

What prevents the type of situation in which the speaker captures the attention of his audience and listeners, in turn, respond with interest—the two-way process which builds toward mutuality of understanding, enrichment, and pleasure?

It is not lack of ability on the part of the children nor a measure of the capacity of the teacher. It is neither unavailability of first-hand experiences nor dearth of reading materials. Surely it is not lack of opportunities nor, indeed, endless repetition of the experience.

Among various possible answers, two are worthy of emphasis. Reporting and making speeches are difficult forms of communication and, sad to say, are often taken for granted as "just natural" for children and dismissed with a brief, "read and report."

The difficulties are manifold. To be successful, the pupil (granting he has something to say) must speak with a degree of clarity; handle the mechanics of speaking so he can be heard and understood by all; make an appeal to a group already organized into a social and emotional pattern of which he is ignorant; interest all of his classmates although their backgrounds and abilities are varied. In addition, he must keep in mind his teacher, whose approval he would win. Small wonder that he gets tangled in his thoughts and forms of expression, and falls back on "ands," "uhs," and "ahs."

Nor are the difficulties limited to the moments of speaking. The pupil must prepare. This means reading, perhaps from a variety of sources, selecting what he wishes to use, combining items into an organized whole, making notes or outlines, familiarizing himself with the accomplished work. This represents an astonishing array of skills not one of which is easy to achieve. What is more reasonable than to take refuge in words, long and impressive, copied from books!

Clearly children need help both in the preparation of reports and speeches and in the act of speaking. Furthermore, they must learn how to evaluate their performance and how to receive suggestions from teacher and peers. This is necessary if growth is to occur. Mere repetition is not enough. Indeed, it may only confirm bad habits.

How better can a teacher help children than to keep alive in their minds the understanding that talking (in this case, reporting and making speeches) is communication and of little value unless it brings about a meeting of minds, at least to some extent? In other words, one speaks because he has something to share; others listen that they may learn.

For the best results, reading materials used in preparation need to be varied in type (for interest's sake) and graded in difficulty (to allow for range of abilities) . Direct study is needed of the skills used in locating material, organizing it, taking notes and making outlines.

Helpful suggestions on preparing reports for a program are made by Burrows.[1] These come in the form of photostatic copies of three checklists showing individual help given or needed during preparation, jobs to be done the last two days, and notes for final program. With speeches and reports, Tidyman and Butterfield[2] include other forms of talking used in speaking to groups, for example, explanations and directions, announcements and advertisements, interviews, with help given on each. *Language Arts for Today's Children*[3] helps teacher and pupils differentiate between the demands made by a familiar group and a large, unfamiliar audience.

In this book, methods of teaching reporting and making speeches are built around five examples from children. How they came to be is indicated and comments and queries are offered as to the effectiveness of the teaching procedures used. The exact teaching patterns which emerged will fit no other situation precisely. They may, however, suggest other patterns to be worked out in other groups and offer specific methods which would be suitable for use in other places.

WONDERS OF THE SKY
(Reports)

Sue's report: My report is on the moon. The moon is made up of high, high mountains and low valleys. The mountains are jagged and life is impossible there. There are no plants nor any kind of life on the moon. On the sunny side the temperature is 200-and-some-odd degrees but on the low side it's way below zero.

Mary's report: I am from the meteor group. Meteors go through the air more than 40 miles per second. Some are small as pebbles and others are very large. Two of the largest meteors have landed in Greenland and South Africa. The one that landed in Greenland

---

[1]Alvina Preut Burrows, *Teaching Children in the Middle Grades* (Boston: D. C. Heath & Co., 1952) , pp. 124-27.

[2]Willard F. Tidyman and Marguerite Butterfield, *Teaching the Language Arts* (New York: McGraw-Hill Book Co., 1951) , pp. 216-35.

[3]National Council of Teachers of English, Commission on the English Curriculum, *Language Arts for Today's Children* (New York: Appleton-Century-Crofts, 1954) , pp. 116, 117, 123-25.

weighed about 40 tons and the one that landed in Africa was 10 feet long.

Kenneth's report: Comets have been the mystery of mankind through the years. Many years ago people thought that comets brought evil and war but today we know this is not true. Halley's comet, scientists think, is the biggest one ever known. Its tail was thousands of miles long. The earth went through the tail of Halley's comet, but nobody was hurt.

Harry's report: I am from the stars group. This is my report. My first question is, "Which is the nearest star?" Our nearest star, though not usually called a star, is what we call our sun. To show you how far this is, if you were going in a plane 300 miles per hour it would take you many, many years to get there. My second question is, "Do stars grow?" The answer to this is, "Yes they grow in brightness, then become dimmer again. Scientists think this is caused by a certain pulsation inside the star. While they are growing, a certain ring of green light hangs around them. This is some sort of gas. We have not found out what it is yet."

HOW THEY CAME TO BE

After writing and telling imaginary stories (pp. 24, 28), pupils in room 204 divided into small groups as they continued to think about the wonders of the sky, in connection with their astronomy unit.

First they decided what they wanted to study: the moon, meteors, comets, and stars. Then on the basis of first, second, and third choices of what they wanted to study they formed four groups, trying to keep them somewhat comparable in size.

The class decided that each group would read and discuss what was important to remember. In the end, one person would be chosen from each group to make a report to the class. The report would be practiced in the small group before it was shared in the larger group. The report was to be neither written nor memorized, but made from notes.

At this point, a period was spent studying matters related to form —saying simply and directly what one has in mind, letting each sentence stand on its own feet (avoiding run-ons), speaking so that one can be heard, trying to interest the listeners.

Each group chose a chairman whose duty it was to lead discussion and take a vote when necessary. Each person was to be responsible for his own paper, pencil, and the material he would read. It was understood that the groups would probably continue for several days.

Since the room had built-in desks, the children had to reseat themselves in order to be near their group members. When discussion was going forward, they had to turn and lean in order to hear and be heard.

While the work was progressing, Mrs. Moore circulated among the groups, offering help as needed. Near the close of each period she helped each group mark the point where it was stopping and note where it would start next time.

After working four periods, the reports were shared in science class. (See p. 50.)

After each report, members of the group represented had opportunity to add ideas not mentioned and the whole class participated in discussion, raising such questions as, "Why can't we see stars in the daytime?" and "What about sun spots?"

In the end, each had learned from all and all from each. Put in another way, each was a producer at one point and a consumer at many points.

COMMENTS AND QUERIES

What are the values of small-group work, on appropriate occasions, over a total class experience? What are the chances of getting total participation in contrast to enlisting the active thought of only the most outspoken ones? What personal and social values can be won from the experience of leading a discussion; of voting; of representing a group when reporting?

What are the advantages of having a variety of materials read, thought about, and reported on, in contrast to basic materials read by all? When would the latter be desirable? What difficulties must be faced in using a variety of materials?

Movable furniture is conducive to work in small groups—conducive but not absolutely necessary, as demonstrated by Mrs. Moore. Did the values achieved outweigh the inconvenience experienced? Mrs. Moore thought so.

Hearing the four reports read will help children understand what makes reporting interesting and how planning and practicing what one is going to say makes for smoothness in speech.

DATES AND PLACES
(Report)

He was born in 1730 and lived for sixty-four years. And . . . uh . . . he was born in Germany and . . . uh . . . was a German-American soldier. He was in the Prussian army . . . uh . . . for almost twenty years and he came to America in 1778. And . . . uh . . . he was a good . . . a . . . he trained people in the army a lot and . . . uh . . . he was a good commander, too and he was made Inspector-General and at the last part of his life, he was in Utica, New York. And . . . uh . . . there's a monument in his memory. And . . . uh . . . that's all I could find out about him.

HOW IT CAME TO BE

What teacher does not know the report loaded with dates, places, and words without meaning either to the listener or the reporter—report copied from a book!

Such was Carol's report, and the pupils responded in kind—fiddled with their pencils, looked bored, slumped in their seats.

Letting Carol hear a tape recording of her report was all that was needed to produce results. "I didn't know I talked like that," she exclaimed. A moment later she added, "I guess I didn't know what I was talking about. It wasn't very interesting."

Members of the class agreed and told Carol some of the things they would like to have heard—the man's name, what the man was like as a boy, what kind of family he had, how he got over to this country. Carol responded by saying, "I'm going to make another report. And it's going to be good." Whether or not she succeeded can be judged by a report which she made several weeks later (p. 54).

COMMENTS AND QUERIES

There was no criticism of this unsatisfactory report by the teacher; rather, reliance was placed on the tape recording to help Carol do her own evaluation. The pupils suggested not what was wrong but what they wished they had heard. Carol drew her own conclusions and made plans for the future.

Mr. Jenkins, the teacher, did not approach the run-on sentence directly, but relied on listening to the tape recording, using pupil evaluation, social pressure, and better preparation to lead to smoother talking. Do you think the report "Town Criers" justified his procedure?

Children will easily see themselves in "Dates and Places." Hearing this read may lead to the tape recording and study of their own reports. It should be followed immediately by "Town Criers" in order that the progress made by Carol can be sensed.

TOWN CRIERS
(Report)

Many years ago most towns in Europe had a town crier. He informed the people about the news. The custom was brought over to the United States. Here in Central City, Colorado, during the summer festivals when an opera begins, a town crier goes up and down the streets calling that the opera shall begin.

Another interesting story about the town crier is in one of Richard Wagner's operas, *Die Meistersinger*. A man would play the role of a town crier and every night he would call:

> *Hört ihr Herrn und lasst euch*
> *Die Glock hat zwölf geschlagen sagen.*
> *Dreht aus das Feuer und das Licht,*
> *Damit euch nichts böses geschicht.*
> *Lobet Gott, den Herrn!*

This means:

> *Hear you men and let us tell you,*
> *The clock has struck twelve.*
> *Turn out the fire and the light,*
> *That no evil may befall you.*
> *Praise God, the Lord!*

Today we do not have as many town criers as we used to have, because of our radio, TV, and newspapers that bring us the news. In the future years there probably will be no town criers any more.

HOW IT CAME TO BE

Considerable time passed following the report "Dates and Places" (p. 53), and the teacher was beginning to wonder whether Carol was making any improvement. "Dates and Places" was read by the teacher. All the children remembered it. But no one, not even Carol, knew whose it was, perhaps because the report had been so nondescript and was related so slightly to the reporter.

When the teacher identified the report, Carol spoke quickly, "I can do better than that now." "What would you like to report on?" the teacher asked. "Town criers," she replied, influenced by an article read recently and the fact that her parents had once lived in Germany.

After days of preparation, rereading the article and talking with her parents, Carol made her report. (See p. 54.)

A marked degree of attentiveness replaced the signs of disinterest and restlessness evidenced in connection with the earlier report. A discussion followed:

Teacher: What did you think of Carol's report?

Evelyn: I think she did it very well and I think she made it interesting by using the German.

Teacher: Anything to add?

Jane: It wasn't like the last report when she said "uh" so many times.

Teacher: I noticed that, and I want to point out that when you're talking even though it seems like hours to you when you feel your tongue is going to be tied up with an "and" or an "ah" or a "well," just stop. It won't take more than a second before you can start right in where you left off. Your audience will probably think you stopped on purpose. *(Turning back to the report.)* How do you account for such an excellent report?

Stephen: She talked about something she knew. She had been to Central City.

Carl: She could hear her father and mother talk about it.

Evelyn: Carol had so much interest in it. *(To Carol.)* What books did you read?

Carol: I didn't find any very good books, but the article I read was in the last copy of *Junior Scholastic*.

Teacher: How did Carol make her subject seem near to us and not just a report? *(And, when no answer came.)* Carol didn't leave the crier in Europe. She brought him to Central City, a place we know something about. In other words, she made a transition from Europe to Central City.

Had there been any doubt about the success of the report, the teacher would have been reassured by spontaneous remarks of the children. "That was fun," said one of the new pupils. "Why can't we have more reports?" queried Keith. "I learned a lot," the teacher heard Herbert say. As for the teacher, he waits to hear the new word "transition" on the lips of his pupils.

COMMENTS AND QUERIES

"If at first you don't succeed ... " is the motto of this teacher. The first report, entirely unsatisfactory, was allowed to pass without scolding or chiding. Furthermore, a way was provided for Carol to discover her own lack, and a second opportunity was given. Not only Carol but every member of the class could see the difference between the two reports—and they liked the second one.

Children should hear "Dates and Places" and "Town Criers" in quick succession, in order to detect the marked contrast between a good and a poor report.

STUDENT COUNCIL
(Speech)

I am June Kent and I am from the sixth grade. I came to tell you about a Student Council that we are going to have. We hope that every one will help us. One way in which you can help us, if you want to, is to select your own representatives. Each room should have two representatives. These people should have experience and be able to know what they are doing for at times they may have to be called away from their work. If you have any problem or question, take it to your student-council representative and he or she will bring it up at the Student Council. Sometimes, to children of your age, the word "representative" is rather confusing. This is what it means. A representative is someone chosen to take your place at a meeting for not every one can come because sometimes they would make it too many people.

HOW IT CAME TO BE

Miss Carter was transferred to the new Hunter School in the middle of the year. With her went half of her sixth grade boys and girls to be merged with an equal number selected from various other adjacent schools. Those who had been working with Miss Carter were accustomed to taking the initiative, deciding important issues, carrying some responsibility for their room and building. Other members of the new group brought with them types of response as varied as the situations from which they had come, ranging all the way from the complete obedience pattern to an irresponsible kind of laissez-faire reaction. Building group unity was the first problem to be tackled—as Miss Carter recognized at once.

The opportunity par excellence was offered when the principal asked if the sixth grade, by virtue of its position in the school and the maturity of its members, would take responsibility for helping with a number of school problems—safety, health, patrol, building, cafeteria, and student council. The students were no less pleased than the teacher and plans were soon in progress.

Miss Carter thought of these projects not as extracurricular undertakings, but as the heart of her social science and language arts. Time could, therefore, be spent on the activities without feeling that the so-called "basic subjects" were being slighted.

The children were divided into six small groups (5 or 6 per group) according to interest. Work began, each group studying materials discovered by them and their teacher. Each group had a chairman and secretary. The duties of the former were to lead discussion as needed, put motions, and keep the job clear. The business of the secretary was to make notes of anything that needed to be remembered or referred to the teacher. The aim of each group was to report, eventually, to the whole class the results of their study. The reporters were to be chosen by the groups.

The student-council group was the first to engage the thought of the whole class, because the council needed to be formed as early in the year as possible. The group was not ready to make a report to the class. They needed help on how to proceed.

The teacher saw this as an opportunity for work by the total class. They studied the purposes of a student council. They thought about democratic processes and due representation. They learned to put a motion and respond in a voting situation. Very important was their consideration of the problem of informing other groups of the proposed student council, explaining the matter of representation and securing cooperation.

It was decided, finally, that speeches should be made in each of the other rooms and discussion carried on, if the listeners had questions. This would require work, since the speaking must be of such character as to convey thought and win support for the project.

Members of the student-council group saw clearly that this was a time for planning and decided they could best help themselves by talking with each other, making notes of what they wanted to say and having a tryout period when they would get suggestions from the class for improving their speeches.

After that was done, the six members of the student-council group asked if they might write and practice their speeches. This they did. However, when they went on their tour they spoke spontaneously, all notes and papers left behind. June went by choice to a second grade and delivered the speech reported on page 56.

In delivering this speech, June showed much poise and commanded the attention of the children. Sensing the possible difficulty of second graders with the word "representatives," she prepared an explanation. For June, this was an important experience since it put at her command a new word and one entirely right for the occasion. That it was more than a passing experience is suggested by her remark to Miss Carter, "My voice sounded funny on that word." Her tone and manner in making the remark seemed to imply, "But I'm glad I did."

The last sentence of June's speech is involved and incorrect. Miss Carter recognized this from the tape recording but let the matter pass temporarily. This she did for two reasons—the second graders seemed to understand what June meant and June might easily have had feelings of success turned to defeat by correction at this moment. Later Miss Carter thought she might play the recording again and see if June could correct herself, as, for example, "A representative is someone chosen to take your place at a meeting. Not every one can come because sometimes there would be too many people."

The Student Council for the whole school was formed and, through its representatives from each of the grades, functioned in connection with all the other projects—safety, health, patrol, building, and cafeteria.

Work of all of the sixth-grade committees continued throughout the year as need arose. Although the projects were considered in the fields of social science and language, they did not represent the total program of either.

In what ways is the building of group unity basic in a teaching situation? Did Miss Carter choose an effective means for this purpose? Was she right in thinking of the student-council project as part of her social science program? As language arts?

Always a teacher must decide when to correct form and when to let it pass. Miss Carter was guided by a desire to keep her pupils talking and wanting to use language purposefully. She was letting an incorrect, run-on sentence pass, but with plans for future work on it.

It is worthy of note that form (particularly the run-on sentence) was studied while the speeches were being prepared. Originally, June's first and last sentences were run-ons. Both were corrected. In the final speech (tape recorded), June remembered to handle her first sentence correctly but in the last lapsed into her original run-on. Miss Carter thought it wise to have June correct herself if possible and to do it later rather than at the moment when success in the total experience was being sensed.

Considerable teaching accompanied the planning and delivery of speeches. Many errors were thus corrected before the speeches were delivered and tape recorded. Teacher and pupils were accordingly rewarded by effective speeches worthy of praise instead of shabby results fit only for criticism.

"Student Council" and "Cafeteria Trouble" should be read consecutively to the children, since they belong in the same situation. Each helps in the understanding of the other.

CAFETERIA TROUBLE
(Speech and discussion)

Leader: I'm here to talk to you about the cafeteria. We think you should usually clean your plates because there is so much food wasted. We would like to hear what you think about it.

Beth: A lot of kids got the idea that they could say they're allergic to things. One girl said she was allergic to everything on her plate and I don't think that's possible.

Harry: Yesterday nearly everyone was allergic to peas and the day before nearly everyone was allergic to scalloped potatoes.

Larry: I'd clean my plate if I could have just what I wanted to eat.

Judy: Yes, but he don't want anything but cake and ice cream.

Jimmy: Vegetables are good for you. You should eat them all.

Leader: What should we do, then?

Robert: Some of the kids say they don't have to eat at home—their mothers don't make them eat and we shouldn't.

Mary: If they don't eat their food, I think they should be sent to the nurse and see what's wrong.

Donna: We should ask the nurse to make them bring a note from home about it.

Leader: Is there anything more you want to say?

Larry: I don't think you can clean your plate if you talk too much.

Frances: Everybody's trying to talk at the same time and I am one of them.

Leader: What can we do about it?

Frances: I'm going to pipe down and I think some of the other people should too.

Leader: I'll take these ideas back to the sixth grade and we'll see what can be done about them.

HOW IT CAME TO BE

It happened while the whole class was working on a science unit that trouble arose in the cafeteria. Children were failing to clean their plates and much food was being wasted. This condition was reported to the all-school student council, recently formed, and referred from there to the sixth-grade, cafeteria committee for study.

Members of the group followed the same procedure as was used by the student-council committee (p. 56) and came out with speeches to be delivered to all the rooms in the building. Jim's speech in third grade turned out to be but a brief introductory announcement, followed by discussion in which he was the leader. (See p. 59.)

When all the speeches had been delivered and the ideas of all the children were at hand, the committee reported to the Student Council. The Council, in turn, decided that posters should be made for the cafeteria, one for each room, bearing the question, "How much has your room improved?" Space was to be provided for a daily answer—"None," "Some," "Much." An appointed host or hostess at each table was to be responsible for reporting to the Student Council what should be recorded each day.

Naturally, there was no complete solution to the problem immediately. There were those who complained of this, didn't like that, and in various ways kept their tables from making distinct progress. Sensitivity to the problem was created, however, and the progress which was made represented the thought and responsibility of the children for their own behavior. The time came, and not too slowly, when they could forget completely that they had ever had a clean-your-plate problem.

COMMENTS AND QUERIES

Miss Carter and her pupils spent much time on communication as related to all-school projects. Was it time well spent? Miss Carter thought so. Not only did the children help set and achieve standards, they had an opportunity to feel the reality of many of the concepts and practices they verbalized in social science. They also had an opportunity to use language in situations where they wanted to get results. They were under the necessity of speaking clearly (to be understood) and as interestingly as possible (to capture attention).

The outcomes of the type of teaching-learning experiences described here cannot be measured immediately nor ever completely. In this case, there were hints as to what was happening—the "glistening faces" of the children as they spoke of "our" room and "our" school to guests and pointed to the shining tables with "not a scratch on them"; the growing tendency of the children to take responsibility for sponging the cafeteria floor when they spilled something; picking up papers; using foot scrapers before entering the building; verbalizations which came at the end of the year, such as, "And we did pass our building on as good as it was when we got it."

It remained for June to put her thoughts into verse form and leave the paper on the teacher's desk without comment.

You walk down the halls,
They smell so new,
And wonder how this good fortune,
Ever came to you.

The classrooms are beautiful,
The teachers are, too,
It seems too funny,
They're so nice to you.

Easy, easy,
Careful with fun,
This building's to last
For years to come.

It doesn't take long,
For the years to fly,
And sometime soon,
You'll look back with a sigh.

Those years aren't easily forgotten,
No, not at all,
And some day you'll remember when
You first walked down
That long, long hall.

Definite outcomes of the all-school projects (student council, cafeteria, health, patrol, safety, and building) were apparent when, a year later, Miss Carter could say to new committees formed in her sixth grade for the same projects, "We give you a new building."

4

Dramatizing

What fun it is to sail air-borne
To the land of make-believe,
To be king for a day, or queen, maybe!
Such freedom to achieve!
Then back again to earth-bound ways,
Richer by far for journey made;
Back again to here-and-now,
Content in role to be played.

SEEING IS BELIEVING. ANY TEACHER WHO HAS MADE SPONTANEOUS, creative dramatics a part of his classroom experiences needs no one to convince him of the worth of such activities. He has seen with his own eyes boys and girls grow not only in skills of communicating thoughts and feelings but in understanding themselves and their social relationships.

Consider "The King's Toothache" (p. 65) and the values which came to a class of individuals, with not a little tendency to bicker among themselves. Here was an opportunity to be aggressive in fun, to speak in mode other than regular classroom style ("idiotic old fossil," "bearded billy goat"), but at the same time to be under the necessity of working with others to make the play the thing. Here everyone did his part—nor considered the king more favored than the menial or the writer of invitations—all for "our class play."

It may be the teacher has seen a group of inhibited children turn into happy, spontaneous creatures through play-acting. He may recall a situation in which a deprived sort of child gained stature in

63

his own eyes as well as in the estimation of his peers by being king for a day. He may remember individuals like the potato lady ("Nail Soup," p. 72), older than others and insecure, gain regard for herself. He may visualize the show-off, the aggressor, in the role of the cat ("King's Toothache," p. 65), learning to act in a way that is consistent with the rest of the play and players.

Along with personal and social gains like these, the skills in communication take their place—making the audience understand a character through talking as well as acting; striving for clarity in expression; using single words and phrases as well as sentences to express one's thoughts; ad-libbing when necessary; choosing picture-building words.

Teaching children to express themselves through dramatization can be on a highly professional level or on the level of an amateur. That is to say, a teacher will profit mightily by special training in this field. Without it, however, he can begin where he is and move on from there, getting help from experience and from books, three of which are mentioned on the following pages.

Even the teacher who feels undramatic and awkward need not deny children the fun of dramatics and the learning which goes with it, because he is among the uninitiated. It is not necessary for him to be the "Cat" in the "King's Toothache" nor to become the irate "Potato Woman" tricked by the gypsy and his nail soup. The children can do the acting, and will, if given the opportunity.

Children need guidance, to be sure. They can, however, with comparatively little help (and no demonstration), learn to plan and execute simple dramatics—often without costumes and properties —on their own.

In most instances, it is wise to keep the play in oral form, hence fluid and growing. The mechanics of writing erect a barrier which tends toward rigidity of text, unless the participants are good writers and much time is allowed by the teacher for necessary revisions.

Books and magazines furnish an abundance of material in ready-made plays which can be used creatively. Collections of short stories and readers abound in stories suitable for dramatization. All the activities of the day suggest dramatic possibilities.

Three plays, developed creatively by children and captured stenographically, follow. With each of these come suggestions as to how they came to be and the significance they have for teaching. These suggestions offer not a day-by-day procedure to be followed, but ideas that can be used at any time, wherever children are having fun in play-acting.

THE KING'S TOOTHACHE[1]
(Dramatization based on a ready-made play)

Announcer: We, the sixth graders of room 202, are going to share a play about the king of Icecreamia. We found this play in a reader and have made it over to suit ourselves. All three scenes will be in the throne room. Now, on with the play!

SCENE ONE

(Curtain opens)

Menial: What's the matter, fool?

Jester: You'd better hurry and get out of here. He's in a murderous mood. He just kicked the cat.

Menial: Who, the king?

Jester: Yes. I have never seen him in such a state.

Menial: Saints preserve us, what's wrong?

Jester: I don't know. He's got a pain where nobody ever had a pain before.

Menial: A pain? Where is the pain?

Jester: In his tooth.

Menial: What! In a tooth? Nobody ever has a pain in a tooth. A tooth is a bone and a bone can't hurt.

Jester: It must be a new kind of disease. I'm telling you you'd better get out of here.

Menial: Sh! Here he comes.

King *(entering)*: Oh! My tooth, my tooth! What's the matter with my tooth? Oh! I'll go crazy. I'll go mad. What are you standing there for, you pair of idiots? Do something to stop this pain.

Jester: What can we do, Your Majesty?

King: What do I care what you do? Get this pain out of my face.

Jester *(to menial)*: Go get the soothsayer. He's no good, but he might help.

[1] Wording created by children based on the original text from Beryl Parker and Paul McKee, *Highways and Byways*. Boston: Houghton Mifflin Company, 1938.

King: Oh, oh, it's killing me!

Jester: Now be patient, Your Majesty. He'll soon be here.

King: Who'll be here?

Jester: The soothsayer. He'll make you well with his magic.

King: That bearded old billy goat! What can he do? Ouch!

Jester: There, there, your Majesty! He will be here any minute.

SCENE TWO

Soothsayer *(entering):* Are you in pain, Sire?

King: No, you idiotic old fossil.

Soothsayer: And now let me see. What can I do?

King: You can get this pain out of my face before I go crazy. What are you waiting for? Take it out.

Soothsayer: Well, I can take it out of your jaw, but I'll have to find some place to put it. I couldn't just leave it floating around in the air.

King: All right. Put it anywhere you want. Just get it out of my face.

Soothsayer: Now, let's see. Where would be the best place to put it? *(Cat enters, purrs, rubs against the soothsayer)*

Soothsayer: Aha!

King: What are you "aha-ing" about?

Soothsayer: We can put it there.

King: Where?

Soothsayer: In the c-a-t.

Cat: Meow!

Soothsayer: Here puss, puss. *(To King):* Now hold on to him while I prepare my magic.

> Toothache, make thee now a bee-line,
> Lodge in yonder purring feline.

King *(clapping hand to jaw):* It's gone, Soothsayer. I never would have believed it. You are a pretty fair wizard.

Soothsayer: It's still in the room somewhere. Watch the c-a-t.

Cat *(jumping into the air at the sound of thunder and flash of lightning):* Yeoww! Woww! *(Lying on back with four legs in air, moaning and howling):* Yeoww! Yeoww!

King: How long will he keep that up?

Soothsayer: 'Til we take the pain away, Your Majesty.

King: That's a fine how-do-ye-do. Here I am the honorary head of the Royal Society for the Prevention of Cruelty to Animals and such things go on right in my own palace. Take the pain out of that cat, you animal tormentor! Why, upon my word, I ought to report you.

Soothsayer: I'll have to put it back in your jaw again.

King: Never mind! As if I couldn't stand a little pain. Am I a child? Go on! Hurry up! Do something!

Soothsayer: Yes, Your Majesty.

> Pain, which power of darkness serves,
> Ride again the royal nerves.

(Cat becomes calm and stops in the middle of a yowl)

King: Oh! It couldn't have been as bad as this before. It couldn't have been. Oh! Take it away.

Soothsayer: Shall I put it back in the cat, Your Majesty?

King: No! Let that cat alone. Here I pay you good wages, and you can't even take a pain out of my face.

Soothsayer: I suppose I could put it in an inanimate object.

King: Put it here, put it there, only get it out of my face.

Soothsayer: I shall put it in that table, Sire.

> As readeth the ancient fable,
> A cat may look at a king.
> A pain may lodge in a thing
> So—toothache into the table!

(At the sound of thunder and flash of lightning, the table jumps into the air and flies into bits)

King: Now see what you have done. That table was a family heirloom. Why, it was on that table that Ronald the Bloody signed the death warrant of . . . Ow!

Soothsayer: Sorry, Your Majesty!

King: Sorry! Listen! Either you get this pain out of my head or you'll lose yours.

Soothsayer: Have mercy, Sire, my head won't do you any good.

King: All right! Then use it, and you'll keep it on that skinny neck of yours. Can you get rid of this pain?

Soothsayer: No, Your Majesty.

King: What! You admit it? You have the barefaced effrontery . . . the unmitigated temerity . . .

Soothsayer: Oh, Sire, I beg of you, have mercy. What good will my poor ugly head do you? Let me call in a foreign wizard. He will take away the pain. He is more powerful.

King: A more powerful wizard? I thought you told me when you applied for the job you were the most powerful wizard in the world.

Soothsayer: I am. But, Your Majesty, the foreign wizard is a specialist.

King: Stop talking! Get him!

Soothsayer: He's here, Your Majesty. I took the liberty of sending for him. He's outside now.

King: What! Ho, guards! Bring in the foreign wizard.

SCENE THREE

Foreign Wizard *(an American dentist, accompanied by two guards, enters carrying a large suitcase):* Where's the patient? Give me some light.

King *(groaning in pain):* Oh, oh, oh!

Foreign Wizard *(pushing a bottle under the nose of the king):* Smell this! Inhale, please!

(Foreign wizard examines contents of suitcase. First he brings out a hammer, holds it up where the audience can see it, then shakes his head and returns it to the suitcase. This he does also with a saw. Finally, he brings out enormously large pincers and looks at them. He nods in approval, goes to the king who is sitting on his throne, seats himself astride the king's lap [back to audience] *and makes motions of pulling very hard. At last he leaps to his feet and holds aloft the pincers with something in them* [carved piece of potato] *which looks like a huge tooth.)*

King: How tired I am. I dreamed I was up in a balloon. The pain's gone. I never would have believed it. *(Excitedly):* What's that you're waving around?

Foreign Wizard: That's your tooth.

King: Upon my word, you shall be richly rewarded. Such magic has never before been known. You shall have gold and precious jewels and you will have a place of honor in my palace.

Foreign Wizard: No, no, no! My fee is $5, plus traveling expenses. I will mail you a bill at the first of the month and you can have

your secretary send me a check. I must be leaving. Wash out
your mouth with salt water every hour.

King: What! You want to leave? You refuse these honors?

Foreign Wizard: My good friend, I have an enormous practice
in the country I come from. They need me there.

King: Can nothing make you stay?

Foreign Wizard: No, unless the toothache becomes so prevalent that
I could work up a good practice here. In that case, I might be
willing to stay.

King: You mean that all my subjects would have to have toothache?

Foreign Wizard: No, only about three-fourths of them—the way it
is where I live.

King: No, your price is too great.

Foreign Wizard: In that case, I'll be going. Good-by!

(Foreign wizard leaves accompanied by the two guards)

King *(in high spirits):* Come one, come all! I want to show you
the place where the tooth was.

(Curtain closes)

HOW IT CAME TO BE

Mr. Gibson discovered that his sixth graders were afraid of dramatization. A little investigation showed they had not engaged in
that type of communication in the earlier grades save on a few
occasions when they had memorized short plays for programs. Mr.
Gibson wanted these boys and girls to have the experience of entering
creatively into a dramatic situation and communicating their
thoughts and feelings spontaneously to their listeners. Also, he
wanted to build group unity. How could these things be brought to
pass?

First, he talked to the pupils about the informal aspects of dramatization such as imitating a person, pretending or play-acting in
telling a story or in conversation. The new insights which resulted
brought relaxation and eased the feeling of reluctance about dramatic
activities.

A day later, he asked the boys if they would like to act out the
ball game they had recently played. They need not talk. This was
something new and fun too. Eagerly they took their places in the
front of the room and as eagerly and unselfconsciously pitched,

batted, caught, and made bases. It was their own suggestion to repeat it with another group and use words as well as action.

The next day there was a discussion about the three kinds of dramatizations which might be done—a ready-made play found in a book or magazine; a story read or heard; a personal experience or happening.

Quickly and understandably they voted for the first. But what play would they dramatize? Several said they had plays at home they could bring. Nothing, however, came of this. At last it was suggested that they look through various readers, with the result that three different plays were proposed for use.

Each of the plays was read dramatically with pupils representing chosen characters. In the end a heavy vote was cast for "The King's Toothache."

Characteristically, the boys and girls began at once to think of costumes and properties—red and gold throne room, soothsayer's paraphernalia, a jumping table, black Halloween suit for the cat.

Sensing this as a false lead because it suggested emphasis on externals rather than on characters and how they acted, felt, and thought, the teacher held these ideas in reserve and guided the children toward making choices for members of the cast.

The children proposed that each of them read a speech of his favorite character as a tryout. This proved to be quite undramatic since the person speaking was neither responding to nor addressing anybody. The teacher let this form of tryout continue, making a mental note, however, that another time he would have children in small groups read selected parts of the play.

With little trouble, members of the cast were chosen—king, soothsayer, cat, dentist, announcer, guards, menial and jester—under the stimulation of the question as to what kind of person was suitable for each of the roles.

The teacher had intended that the players would use the text as a guide, feeling free to add or subtract what seemed natural and appropriate to them and the situation. He had no thought of memorized speeches, save possibly the rhymes. This point of view he did not communicate to the pupils, however. In the press of duties the play was simply laid aside for several days.

Imagine his surprise when, on returning to the project, he found speeches partially, almost wholly, memorized. His job now was to help the children ease themselves into the characters and to forget word-for-word speeches. This he did by asking such questions as, "If you were the king, what would you do? What would you say?" He asked that books be left on desks, thus encouraging improvisation.

Members of the audience proved to be constructive critics, offering suggestions and raising questions about the acting—how real the characters were or what more was needed. They even took turns representing the various characters (acting and talking) until everybody in the room had participated.

Members of the cast now began to work apart from the class, sometimes in the auditorium when they were free from other classroom responsibilities. Sometimes they worked by themselves; more often than not, under the guidance of the teacher.

Since only nine children were needed to play "The King's Toothache," the class suggested that a second cast be chosen. This was done. The remaining 24 members of the class were divided into working groups to prepare scenery and costumes, plan for seating in the auditorium, write invitations, and act as ushers.

The two casts shared their interpretations of the play with five different groups in the building. The last performance, planned for the auditorium, was considered of the greatest importance since special guests were invited. Both casts wanted to play. Finally, it was suggested by the children that the players in the two casts draw lots for the parts. This resulted in five from one group and four from the other.

In spite of the fact that the nine children had never played together before and only thirty minutes remained before the appointed hour, not the slightest confusion was sensed. They played together with a remarkable degree of smoothness and with the type of spontaneity which characterizes a backyard play. No "lines" were forgotten, no prompting was needed, so much had the children identified themselves with the characters they represented, even creating new expressions at that late date. Lights were operated by the children and curtains opened and closed; the table jumped at the appropriate moment and fell crashing to the floor; the cat yowled and howled, and rolled on his back so furiously as practically to steal the show.

The teacher? He sat in the back row, not without his moments of wondering if he had delegated too much responsibility, but well pleased at the way the boys and girls lived freely and happily on the stage—an experience long to be remembered!

The text, of course, is not to be copied, but used to help other groups work out their own interpretations of the original story or handle some other story set up in dramatic form in similar fashion.

Mr. Gibson believes that many values came to his pupils through this experience; for example, skill in understanding and appreciating various characters; freedom in expression and action; ability to use language creatively; growth in working with others; effectiveness in carrying responsibility.

Granting a place for the memorized play, what are the differences in values to be won in spontaneous dramatics over the former?

The principal, walking to his office after the play, said, "I think that this is good for the children. Maybe they ought to have more of it." Do you agree? Are the values great enough to warrant the necessary expenditure of school time on preparation?

"The King's Toothache," in its original form and as worked out by the pupils in Mr. Gibson's class, might be read to, or by, children, as an aid in handling creatively a ready-made play. This process would show where the text was memorized (the rhymes, for example) and where it changed form in the hands of the actors. This or any play might be kept so simple that neither costumes nor properties would be needed—so simple, in fact, that it represents but the passing moment rather than hours of time needed for the achievement of a more or less finished performance.

NAIL SOUP[2]
(Creative dramatization of a story)

Announcer: This story is about something that happened on market day. There was much excitement. People were buying and selling. A gypsy was sitting by a fire, stirring a nail in a pot of boiling water.

---

[2]Eleanor M. Johnson and L. B. Jacobs (eds.), *Adventure Lands.* (In the Read-text series, *Treasury of Literature*) Columbus, Ohio: Charles E. Merrill, 1954.

Vegetable Woman: Onions for sale—delicious fruits and vegetables —they are the best.

Flower Woman: Flowers—green ones—yellow ones—flowers for sale!

Mustache Man: Mustaches for sale—grown mustaches and magnetic ones!

Potato Woman: Big potatoes! Nice potatoes!

Buyer: I'd like to buy a dozen tulips, please.

Flower Woman: Yes Ma'am!

Buyer: I'd like to buy half a dozen petunias, too.

Flower Woman: That will be twenty cents, please.

Mustache Man: Mustaches for sale—grown mustaches and magnetic ones! Anything you want right here!

Buyer: I will have magnetic mustaches, purple and green polka dot.

Mustache Man: That will be twenty-five cents.

Buyer: Okay!

Another Buyer: I would like to have those false teeth.

Buyer *(at another booth)*: Those are good onions. How much?

Vegetable Woman: Six cents.

Buyer: I will take one.

Another Buyer: Do you sell parsley?

Vegetable Woman: Yes.

Buyer: I would like to have some. How much?

Vegetable Woman: That will be six cents.

Woman with onion *(to the gypsy)*: What are you making?

Gypsy: Nail soup.

Woman with onion: M-m-mmm! It is very, very rare.

Gypsy: I got this on my many travels. A little salt will bring out the flavor. Pepper will make it hot. If only I had an onion.

Woman with onion: Please take this one.

Gypsy *(taking onion and putting it into pot)*: Well, thank you!

Woman with parsley: My parsley is better than her onion. Take some.

Gypsy *(taking parsley and putting it into pot)*: Well, thanks a lot!

Potato Woman: Potatoes! Potatoes!

Gypsy *(going to potato woman)*: Those potatoes look good, but I bet they have spots in them.

Potato Woman: Oh no, they haven't got spots inside of them.

Gypsy: Prove it. You'll have to cut them open.

Potato Woman *(cutting potato into halves):* See, it hasn't got spots in it. *(Angrily)* Take it! I can't use it, now!

Gypsy *(putting potato into pot):* Thank you!

Potato Woman *(very angrily):* You are *not* welcome!

Flower Woman: That poor potato woman giving her potatoes to that gypsy! She happens to be my friend, and when she gets mad, she gets mad!

Gypsy: Now I have an onion and parsley and a potato . . .

Meat Man *(running in):* My meat is better than any of them. Take it!

Gypsy *(eating soup greedily):* M-m-mmm, the meat's so delicious and the potatoes so yummy and the onion and parsley—delicious!

Gypsy *(rinsing the pot and carefully saving the nail):* Well, that's all I want. *(Picking up his belongings and moving down the road)* The next town we come to will be the same thing, I hope.

Announcer: And so the story ends and the little old gypsy will go on to the next town with his nail soup.

HOW IT CAME TO BE

Mrs. Grant's children were doing well with storytelling. They had made stories from their own experiences and told those which they had read. An experience made the teacher realize how close the children were to dramatization.

When Millie had finished telling "The Three Billy Goats Gruff," Carol observed, "She dramatized it." "What do you mean?" asked Mrs. Grant in surprise. "She made the characters act with her voice," came the answer. "Where did you learn that word 'dramatize'?" continued the teacher. "In a book," said Carol. "I read it there."

Mrs. Grant had mixed feelings about having dramatizations done in her classroom. She believed in the values which might result, but was fearful of not knowing how to help the pupils plan and carry through such activities. After all, she had never done such a thing nor seen anybody else do it. She had received no special training in the subject though she had been exposed to it in her teacher-education courses. Looking back on her own elementary school days she realized that spontaneous and creative activities were not even used there. Mrs. Grant had another fear. What if the pupils, once free to act and talk as they wished, got out of hand or merely acted silly?

Maybe instead of interpreting characters, the pupils would exaggerate and act smart to cover their embarrassment. And what would she do with pupils who were not playing at the moment, but acting as audience?

With these questions in mind, she did what a growing teacher would naturally do—she sought help. In addition to her language book, she used *Creative Dramatics in Home, School and Community.*[3]

In this book, Mrs. Grant found pages packed with practical suggestions as to steps to be used in initiating children into dramatics—pantomime, characterization, transition into dialogue, transition into stories.

These aids she supplemented by three chapters from *Playmaking with Children*[4]—choosing stories to dramatize; presenting the story; story dramatization.

Mrs. Grant started by doing group pantomime activities. "Who could show us how the crooked man walked down the crooked street?" she asked. When hands waved, she chose 8 or 10 children to be crooked men walking down crooked streets all over the room. "Who can show us how to pick blueberries?" And a bevy of workers stooped low to pick imaginary berries to fill imaginary pails, now and again putting fingers slyly to lips for a delicious make-believe taste. "Maybe each of us could be an ice cream man and call his wares." "Ice cream, ice cream, ice cream!" called out the children.

Time was spent identifying the kinds of dramatic activities in which children engage daily—showing a friend how a movie star walked in a recently seen show; tossing one's head and turning away in disgust when worsted in an argument; stretching up straight and tall when wearing a brand new suit. This opened the way for individual demonstrations, after the pattern, "I could show you how . . ."

Another period was spent reading and talking about the kinds of dramatizations that might be done. The children passed over the idea of play-acting their own experiences, as well as the suggestion of choosing a ready-made play. The vote was clearly for putting into

[3]Ruth Lease and Geraldine Brain Siks, *Creative Dramatics in Home, School and Community.* New York: Harper and Brothers, 1952. Chapter 6.
[4]Winifred Ward, *Playmaking with Children* (New York: D. Appleton-Century Co., 1947), pp. 50-113.

dramatic form some story previously read. "What story can we do?" and "When can we begin?" were the questions which came pressing now.

Talking about the kind of story which would dramatize well, the children decided, under the teacher's guidance, to look for a story which had much action and characters who talked or could be made to talk. The next day they would be ready with their suggestions.

Almost as many stories were proposed as there were children in the class—twenty-three. As the stories were described and promoted by the individual pupils, certain ones gained in favor—five, then two and at last one—"Nail Soup."

At this point, the teacher read the story from beginning to end, stressing its dramatic qualities.

She then followed the technique used in pantomiming by suggesting that many stalls be set up around the room, all open and everybody in the room becoming either a buyer or a seller.

"What would the different stalls sell?" she asked. "Vegetables," answered the children, "flowers, meat." Sellers were chosen and buyers gathered around them. Talking started, each stall working independently. No one felt self-conscious because there was no audience. No one wondered what to say nor tried to remember the words in the book because he was in a situation which he understood, and language took its rightful place.

Gypsy centers were then set up all around the room. Again each child was either a gypsy stirring an imaginary nail in an imaginary pot of boiling water or one who contributed an onion, a potato, a sprig of parsley or a piece of meat to make something substantial of "nail" soup.

The children then seemed ready to play the story from beginning to end. Accordingly, characters were chosen—a gypsy, a potato woman, a seller of meat, a parsley woman, an onion woman and three or four buyers for each stall.

Mrs. Grant urged the children to keep the action going—not bothering too much about words, but speaking as they wished.

The first time through, the playing was rough, but sequence was maintained and some talking done. Within the framework provided, spontaneous talking could now flourish.

A new cast was chosen for the next day and after that still another until every child in the room had participated in representing some character.

Being members of an audience meant not merely sitting and waiting for a playing part, but entering creatively into the play-acting so as to help the present players and to prepare for using one's own turn well.

Different casts went from room to room sharing their new experience, and finally played in their own room to specially invited guests. On that occasion some of the text was remembered from previous playings, some of it created while they were acting. The text, as given on pages 72-74, was recorded stenographically.

The teacher knew the children were learning not to be embarrassed or afraid, but she was happy to hear Dick (one of the shyest) say, "At first I felt funny inside. Then I said to myself, 'The book says you don't have to be afraid' and I wasn't." Feeling somewhat inferior because she was older than her peers and not able academically, the Potato Woman came into adequacy in calling and selling her wares and, incidentally, in winning a laugh from her classmates. Said the children, "She was good the way she got mad at the gypsy." No one in the room who did not know that the pupils had learned (in varying degrees, naturally) how to identify themselves with characters, to talk as they talked and act as they acted— this, in contrast to learning and remembering speeches.

Many things remained to be learned, but Mrs. Grant knew they would come with future attempts at dramatics.

COMMENTS AND QUERIES

Essentially, Mrs. Grant looked not to the finished product as a test of good teaching and learning, though they were nothing of which to be ashamed. She looked at children and tried to estimate what was happening to them as persons as well as what was being achieved in skills of communication. Is this placing emphasis where emphasis is due? Is this a safe criterion for other types of oral communication?

Reviewing the situation, Mrs. Grant was amazed at the number and variety of learnings which became a part of the larger experience of dramatizing "Nail Soup," for example, ad-libbing, working with others, overcoming fear, winning audience response, achieving regard for one's self, reading, listening, evaluating, locating stories in books, imagining oneself in the position of another person, showing honest feelings. "What is true in this instance," said Mrs. Grant to herself, "must be true of any and all teaching situations." A sobering and challenging thought!

So satisfying were the experiences of this teacher, that she decided to have a rack for clothing and a dress-up box in the corner of her room. A hat, a rose, high heels, a trailing skirt—what wonders by them are wrought, touched by the magic of a child's imagination!

"Nail Soup" can be read and compared with the original story as a means of discovering how the children made a play that was their own. It should not be copied but used as an aid in turning other stories into dramatic form.

CHRISTMAS IN MEXICO
(Original play created from experiences)

Setting: Interior of Mexican home (all three scenes)
Characters: Papasita; Mamasita; Pedro (older son); Angel (younger son); Rosita (oldest daughter); Felicia, Juanita, Manuela (younger daughters)

Scene One

(Curtain opens)

Mamasita *(stirring tortillas in one corner of the room):* I wonder when those lazybones are going to get up. I hope they will like these special *tortillas* I am making for their Christmas dinner.
(Papasita and Pedro enter)
Mamasita: Where are you going?
Papasita: To the market.
Mamasita: What time will you be back?
Papasita: Around nine o'clock.
(Sleeping children waken and rise)
Manuela: Can't we go?
Papasita: No, you are too little.
Rosita: Why are you going?
Felicia: Tell us, we won't tell anybody.
Papasita: To market.
Felicia: What are you going to get there?
Papasita: That is a surprise.

All children: Tell us.
Pedro: No.
Manuela: Can't we go?
Pedro: No, you are too little. It is too early in the morning.
All children: Too little!
All: Adios.
  (Papasita and Pedro leave)

Scene Two

Mamasita: Let us get dinner.
Rosita: Do you want me to help you?
Juanita: Mother, I can't find my serape.
Mamasita: Well, look good and maybe you'll find it.
Manuela: I made a clay bowl for Mamasita's Christmas.
Felicia: I made an American bowl.
Juanita: Guess what I made for Pedro—a little clay piggy bank.
  Course it's not so nice as the ones in the market.
Manuela: I made a sombrero for Pedro because his is all worn out.
Rosita: I made one for Papasita, too.
Felicia: There'll be a lot of sombreros.
Angel: I wish I could have a burro for Christmas.
Juanita: You'd look funny on a burro.
Felicia: Come here, Angel. We will pretend riding a burro. It will
  be so much fun.
  (Felicia and Angel do a donkey dance)
Manuela: I wish you would teach me that.
Juanita: I do not want to ride on that kind of burro.
Felicia: I wish Papasita and Pedro would come back.
Rosita: Here they come now.
  (Children run to the door)

Scene Three

  (Papasita and Pedro enter carrying a package)
Children: What have you got?
Pedro *(holding high a stick with a bag swinging on the end of it)*: A
  piñata.
Children: When can we open it? Let's break it now.
Papasita: If you will be quiet we will do it now.

(The children take sticks and try to break the piñata. *Felicia swings and misses.)*

Pedro: You missed it. Watch me.

(Pedro misses too. All laugh. Each child tries and misses the piñata, *on purpose, so that Angel, the littlest one, can break it. The wrapped candy which was in the* piñata *tumbles to the floor and the children scramble to pick it up and put it on plates.)*

Juanita: We must give our aunts and uncles [i.e., the class visitors] some of these goodies from the *piñata.*

(The children run to the front of the stage)

All: Merry Christmas!

(After the curtain closes, the children pass the candy to the visitors)

HOW IT CAME TO BE

The unit on "Life in Mexico" was drawing to a close as the Christmas season approached. Miss Miller wondered how the children could make its culmination most meaningful.

Ever since the day the children had dramatized a story about Pedro and his burro they had been asking, "When can we do it again?" The thought came to Miss Miller that this might be the time for creating a play, drawing for ideas upon the things they had been learning in their social science unit.

Her suggestion met with instantaneous response. It turned out, however, that the children were more willing than able. They had plenty of facts about people, markets, sombreros, *tortillas, piñatas* and the like, but little notion as to how to handle them dramatically.

After a period of general discussion, a committee of five was chosen by the children to work out plans, with the help of the teacher.

The first meeting of the committee proved to be discouraging to the teacher. Nothing emerged around which a play could be built. The children moved from idea to idea and finally lapsed into talking about their own Christmas. The teacher brought them back to Mexico by asking what Christmas would be like there. The *piñata* was mentioned at once and ideas began to flow as to how it could be made part of a play.

The following day the committee started at that point and worked backward to get their action—a *piñata* in a Mexican home, with each member of the family trying to break it—someone going to market to buy it as a surprise—others staying at home—children getting out of bed and talking about Christmas.

When the report came in, the members of the class filled in details eagerly. They would have a family of eight, Pedro the oldest and Angel the youngest. What fun they had thinking of names—Papasita, Mamasita, Rosita, Felicia, Juanita, Manuela! Mamasita could be baking *tortillas* and the children just getting out of bed (crawling from under a blanket on the floor of the stage). Papasita and Pedro would go to market for "the surprise." While they were gone, the rest of the children could have a little talk about Christmas and the presents they were going to give other members of the family. "Felicia" and "Angel" volunteered the information that they could do a donkey dance they had learned in their tap-dancing class.

In the end, the children decided on three scenes—Papasita and Pedro taking off for market while others remain at home, children and mother at home engaging in activities while waiting for the return of Papasita and Pedro, the whole family celebrating the breaking of the *piñata*.

Now the play began. Different boys and girls took the places of various characters in the first scene, acting as they thought the characters would act and talking as they would talk. Incidentally, all of the text had to be created.

Other boys and girls tried out scenes two and three, keeping the action going and letting the talking be as sketchy as must be. Those not acting, at any given moment, served as audience and made suggestions for improvement.

Day by day the scenes grew in richness of detail, in acting and talking, and every child in the room had opportunity to act in the role of his chosen character. Going to the Little Theater was a special treat since there lights could be switched on and off and curtains pulled by invisible but eager hands. For this occasion, a cast was chosen by the children and considerable formality accompanied the performance.

"May we invite people to come and see our play?" begged the children after their first experience on the stage. It so happened that Miss Miller was a member of a college class in child development and at once thought of her classmates as possible guests. Sparring for time until she could check, she answered, "Of course, but let's talk more about that tomorrow."

The next day Miss Miller told the children about the forty men and women preparing to become teachers who would like to see the play. What did they think of that? "Fine!" they responded. "But," they queried, "wouldn't we have to write the play then and learn it?" "No, indeed," was the prompt assurance. "You can go on just as you are now doing."

Up to this time, the play had closed with the breaking of the *piñata*, which was to contain just enough pieces of candy for members of the class. "Now we'll have to have more candy, won't we?" suggested Eddie. "We could pass it around after the play in some of the paper plates we decorated," added Jean. "We must buy the kind of candy that's wrapped so it won't get dirty when it falls on the floor," offered Rosalie. Pearl came forward with the idea that there should be something about the guests "right in the play." "What are we going to call them?" asked Dick. "We can't say 'teachers'." "They're not teachers yet, anyway," volunteered Mary Ann. Finally, they settled on "aunts and uncles," then played the last scene again.

It was presented on the final day to the high amusement of the guests. And what fun the children had, after the curtain was closed, walking among the guests, passing the candy with such gracious words as, "Will you have something from our *piñata?*" "Do take a piece!"

The play was never written, but remained in oral form, changing creatively through each performance. It came into written form, as recorded here, by the services of one of the teachers who was able to capture it stenographically.

COMMENTS AND QUERIES

Miss Miller found special help for her undertaking in *Creative Drama in the Lower School*.[5] Although the examples given there related to primary and kindergarten levels, they did give her a sense of what she might expect from children. The fact that dramatizations could be handled so creatively by younger children gave her increased belief in her fifth-grade boys and girls.

[5]Corinne Brown, *Creative Drama in the Lower School* (New York: D. Appleton & Co., 1929), pp. 37-57.

Miss Miller needed special assurance since, in previous teaching situations, she had thought lines needed to be memorized. Her sense of achievement was great when she found that her pupils were capable of original work and in the process could identify themselves well with characters they were portraying and act without self-consciousness. What a delightful relief from unnatural acting by embarrassed children who were forgetting their lines and leaning on her for prompting!

Later, Miss Miller added to her resources *Creative Dramatics in Home, School and Community.*[6] In this she found many ideas for creative dramatics in the school program—such as language arts, social studies, nature study and science, safety education.

Through a combination of reading and experience, this teacher came to certain basic understandings of what needed to be done for success in original dramatics. This she expressed one day to another inquiring teacher: Select some small part of an experience to dramatize; make a story of it; create characters; give them names and things to do; let the characters live and talk. "It is just as simple as that," she declared. "Try for yourself and see!"

"Christmas in Mexico" can be read to or by children after necessary orientation has been made. This means acquaintance with such words as *piñata,* sombrero, serape, *tortilla,* and knowledge of the fact that this is a play which children created, planning their own climax, happenings, introduction and ending.

"Christmas in Mexico" will be of slight value if it is only learned and played as given here. Its best purpose will be served if it suggests to groups of boys and girls the possibility of putting their own learnings into dramatic form—in other words, making original plays.

[6]Lease and Siks, *op. cit.*

5

Using Words Well

Words have wings
Or feet of clay,
To lift aloft
Or hold us down.
When we can soar
Among the clouds,
Why be content
With earth alone?

THAT CHILDREN SHOULD LEARN TO USE WORDS WELL IS A FOREGONE CON-
clusion. How this can best be done poses a question. Shall the approach be through language, as such, and its varying forms or through
children and the problems they face in attempting to communicate
their thoughts?

This chapter is built around the latter point of view with the
support of research which suggests the superior efficacy of the thought
approach over the grammar approach.[1] In substantiation of this
point of view, it offers ideas and examples built within the following
framework: developing an adequate vocabulary; pronouncing sounds
and syllables correctly; expressing thought clearly and adequately;
developing style; and adding labels.

Effective talking requires attention to vocabulary. Children must
not only master new words, but relearn words or combinations of

---

[1] Mildred A. Dawson, *Teaching Language in the Grades* (Yonkers, N. Y.: World
Book Co., 1951) , pp. 292 ff.

words (always difficult and sometimes unpleasant) which have been learned incorrectly and are now used without question and accepted as right. They must not only develop a general vocabulary, but also a special one for each field in which they study. In this growing store, they must have words—adequate in number and kind—for making their thoughts clear and interesting to their listeners. This is not so much a process of learning and storing up words to be used at some future time, as it is a matter of discovering and meeting needs as they arise in talking.

Pronouncing words clearly and correctly plays an important part in effective communication. This means paying attention to sounds and syllables in order to avoid running them together into an unintelligible jumble. It means, further, watching a variety of common errors, such as failure to speak consonants distinctly and vowels correctly, omission of endings, and slighting part of a blend.

Words and combinations of words are valuable only when they aid in the expression of thought. Sometimes, a single word may carry a complete thought. Many times, a phrase is adequate. Often, however, more is needed. At this point, children, because of vagueness of thought and the difficulties imposed by language, often lose sight of what they are trying to say and wander hopelessly, guided by nothing but a loose chain of associations. The so-called "run-on" sentence results, generously punctuated with "well," "ah," and "uh." The need for learning to stop when a single thought has been expressed or to add a second (and maybe another) by the use of connectives becomes of great importance, though not a matter for extreme pressure. How often even adults come to clarity of thought only after discovering it through fumbling attempts at talking!

Style goes beyond form, important though that may be. It is displayed when children, having something interesting to say, choose appropriate and colorful words, use variety and originality in expression, and maintain a spirit of joy and sparkle in what they are saying sufficient to make their listeners want to hear what they are trying to express. Developing style is a lifelong undertaking with its beginning in childhood.

After children have learned—through sensibility of the ear and flexibility of the tongue—to speak with some degree of effectiveness, grammatical terms come as labels to what is already known through usage, and as a help in future refinement of practices. The exact moment when this should occur is not a matter of agreement. Perhaps the moment is not the same for all groups and all individuals. But research reported by Dawson[2] seems to indicate the time for formal grammar lies at a level higher than the elementary school. However, since some junior high schools expect pupils to have familiarity with grammar upon arrival, some teachers who work by the thought approach like to close their sixth-grade experiences with attention to labels.

Five tape-recorded examples of children talking are now given, with suggestions as to the opportunities they provide for teaching form, followed by comments and queries regarding the efficacy of teaching techniques used. The total pattern of teaching for each example would never be duplicated. Details of the process, however, suggest methods suitable for other groups of children in other places.

AQUARIUS THE WATER CARRIER
(Developing adequate vocabulary)

My horoscope name is Aquarius.

Once upon a time way out in space the Big Dipper, which I suppose you all know, had a flood. It was the worst thing I have ever seen.

It seemed like me and the whole universe were swept into the river. We were held captive for years, it seemed like.

Finally Jupiter, the mightiest of all the planets, told the Dipper to turn us loose. He opened the floodgates and we all fell out in space.

The day after this mishap happened, I floated back to where the Dipper was and he was almost all dried up. So I went over to the Little Dipper which was full almost to the top with water and I got my pail out and started hauling water from the dipper—from the Little Dipper to the Big Dipper. And I haven't stopped yet and that is how I got my name, Aquarius the Water Carrier.

OPPORTUNITIES FOR TEACHING

It is obvious that Jim had learned important words in the field of astronomy which helped him share his thoughts clearly—Aquarius, universe, Jupiter, Big Dipper, Little Dipper, planets. He had learned,

[2]*Op. cit.*, pp. 292 ff.

also, to choose picture-building words as a means of helping his hearers see and feel what he was talking about—floodgates, floated, swept.

Neither of these skills just happened; they resulted from definite effort on the part of pupil and teacher. For example, prior to the telling of science stories by members of the class, a word chart was started. It was made of a large piece of cardboard with spaces blocked off for words, and rested on the chalk trough ready for use. Impor tant words in the field of astronomy, known by the children at the beginning of the unit on planets, were written on the chart, and the list grew as study continued and new words were discovered. Incidentally, the chart was the work of a small group during the art period.

An occasion for on-the-spot teaching occurred in connection with Jim's use of the expression "mishap happened." "What a fine word you used, Jim—'mishap'," said the teacher. "Perhaps you would like to put that on our chart when you have time. I noticed you used the word 'happened' after it. Is that needed or not?" Jim himself found "mishap" in the dictionary and saw it meant "an unlucky accident." "This might just as well read 'an unlucky happening'," the teacher explained. In the end, all saw that the word "happened" was unnecessary.

The expression "seemed like," used twice, was allowed to pass since it is in such common use even with adults, and the teacher wanted to be careful not to overpower a boy who was just getting on his feet. The construction "me and the universe" was allowed to pass, also, since it seemed to convey thought and feeling in this situation even better than "universe and I" would have done. This type of construction will be handled later in connection with such expressions as "me and Jane" and "for Jack and I." They will then be learned through listening to the correct forms in many and varied sentences and contrasting them with the incorrect forms. The children may be helped by the suggestion that no one would say "me went" but rather "I went." Why change it when there are two persons instead of one? No reference will be made to nominative and objective cases; no attempt will be made to indicate the influence of a preposition on the pronoun which follows.

From the standpoint of personal values, it is interesting to know that the recording represents Jim's second attempt. In the first trial he failed miserably, using a few run-on sentences which showed confusion of thought and ended by breaking down entirely. With the encouragement and help of his teacher, he learned how to prepare an imaginary story and was able to tell it in such way as to capture the interest and attention of the entire class.

Mrs. Moore felt a triumph not only for skills achieved but also for a developing boy when Jim lingered after school to say, "I'm not afraid any more; not a bit—and I did put the word on the chart."

COMMENTS AND QUERIES

Mrs. Moore did considerable direct teaching, pointed toward an end, before the moment when stories were to be told. This reduced the number of errors made and increased the points of success. She did some on-the-spot teaching and looked toward the future for further opportunity to help children with needs that were revealed through their efforts at talking.

Jim had been reminded earlier of his tendency to use expressions like "me and the universe." What about the theory of never tolerating an error after it has been studied and corrected? Is it a theory that is possible or even desirable to put into practice?

This teacher believes that growth in language and in personality are inextricably bound together.[3] She was able not only to help Jim improve in skills, but at the same time to keep him wanting to try and doing better with each attempt.

What significance is to be attached to the fact that the boy waited until he was alone with the teacher to tell her he was no longer afraid? Notice that he emphasized it—"not a bit," then added quickly another thought not connected with his feelings. Why did he do that? Why was Mrs. Moore pleased not only at Jim's success but also, and especially, at his ability and willingness to verbalize his feelings?

"Aquarius the Water Carrier" may give encouragement to pupils who have failed or who for a variety of reasons may feel afraid and inadequate. If listened to carefully, it may furnish a valuable opportunity for detecting words that are well chosen and those that are

[3]*Experiencing the Language Arts.* (Prepared at Florida State University.) Tallahassee, Florida: State Department of Education, 1948, pp. 48-55.

not quite right. All the better if the listeners can supply the correct form in each case.

CONTRARY GOAT
(Pronouncing sounds and syllables correctly)

Once upon a time there was a goat. He did everything 'cept what he was 'sposed to do. One day he knocked down a mountain to make a pathway. They didn't like that . . . to get to . . . .

Another time he knocked down the umpire state building because he wanted to get past without goin' around.

They had to do something about this goat. So they decided to shoot it with a cannon ball. But he just bent down his head and hit the ball and it went right back through the cannon and out the other end of it. *(Laughter)*

And so, finally, they used everything but it wouldn't work. So they just left it the way it was. And that was the end.

OPPORTUNITIES FOR TEACHING

Miss Mead was so pleased with this, Danny's first real achievement in storytelling, that she did not want matters of form intruding to destroy the pleasure of the moment sensed not only by her but by Danny and his classmates. She did, however, notice some sounds and syllables which needed attention.

Meanwhile, the children laughed and talked in a kind of informal evaluation. Spontaneously, came such remarks as "Danny had a good idea"; "He made a good story"; "I wish it had been longer"; "I **would like to know** some other things that goat did." Then Bill gave the perfect lead. Said he, "It's empire state building, not umpire state building. An umpire umpires a ball game. I don't know what 'empire' means."

Miss Mead had been helping Danny, privately, on the short vowel sounds in words in which he was having difficulty—git for get, jist for just. Maybe he still could not hear "e" and "u" as different sounds. She started by complimenting Danny for using "get" and "just" correctly, then pronounced clearly for the whole class the two words, "empire" and "umpire." She then asked Danny to pronounce the one which was correct for this situation—empire.

Miss Mead knew the dictionary would not help Bill in getting an answer to his question, since it is "empire state" not "empire" which is important here. "New York," she said to the class, "is called the empire state. This building is in New York, hence the name 'empire state building'."

The skipping of syllables was noticed by no one, possibly because it was so prevalent among members of the class. This matter was allowed to pass, but the teacher was already making plans for study of this problem in the language period the following day. As a take-off, she would call attention to such words as 'cept, 'spose, comin', asking pupils to supply the correct pronunciations with all parts said distinctly—except, suppose, coming. She would also have pupils supply the correct forms for other words in which they slighted syllables. Many examples would be chosen and pronunciations made just slowly enough so that each part would be said, yet rapidly enough to keep the total impression of the word.

Her planning was interrupted at this point by Sandra, who said, "Miss Mead, Danny said that they had to do something about the goat and I don't understand who 'they' are."

Teacher: Who are "they" Danny?

Danny: Oh, the people.

Teacher: What people?

Danny: The ones that didn't like the goat.

Teacher: Yes, maybe the ones who were troubled by his doings. If you tell us that at the first, then you can use the word "they" later and we know what you mean.

Remembering Danny's previous failures and present success, the teacher did not want the occasion to end on a negative note. Including the whole class in her remarks, she said, "Was it not fine that Danny could make all of us enjoy his story and ask for more?" Then looking toward the boy whose cheeks were still flushed with triumph, she added, "That is one of the best tests of using words well in telling a story."

COMMENTS AND QUERIES

Miss Mead is far from believing that the building of skills, as such, much less the correcting of errors, is the whole business of teaching children how to talk. She does believe, however, that in the process of talking children must develop language skills, and that part of the job is the relearning of words or combinations of words which they have learned incorrectly.

Miss Mead agrees with Strickland[4] that developing skills is a continuous process, with no grade-level demarcation possible. Each aspect is to be attacked when need and readiness are demonstrated. She tries to know where her pupils are and to lead on from there. As for errors, she believes that study and practice are for those in need —individuals or the whole class, as the case may be.

Acting in the light of this belief, Miss Mead surveyed her class to discover individual assets which needed encouragement and development, as well as practices which needed correction. This resulted in individual conferences and individual or group help offered when children were talking or in a separate language period. The individual conference she found vastly rewarding and not too time consuming; help during the time of talking was kept at the minimum to avoid discouraging individuals and destroying the meaning of what was being done; work for the language period, as such, grew out of needs detected and suggestions from her course of study.

Miss Mead works on form from the standpoint of thought rather than in terms of grammar. For example, she did not label the last problem touched upon as "pronoun without an antecedent," but spoke in terms of clarity, "We didn't know what you meant."

By comparing and contrasting the work of Danny with that of Annie (p. 92) and Peter (p. 28), one can see that this teacher gives more than lip service to the concept "individualization of instruction." Miss Mead was led to this type of teaching through experience and by reliance on the kind of help furnished by Olson[5] in his graphs showing variations in growth.

This tall tale could serve no better purpose than to make children laugh in enjoyment of humor based on such gross exaggeration, and to give encouragement in creating other foolish actions of a contrary goat. But it does serve, also, as a good springboard for a plunge into the problem of listening for sounds and syllables in the interest of

[4]Ruth G. Strickland, *The Language Arts* (Boston: D. C. Heath and Company, 1951), pp. 145-47.
[5]Willard C. Olson, *Child Development* (Boston: D. C. Heath & Co., 1949), pp. 178-83.

pronouncing words correctly—the exact content to be determined by the practices (good and bad) of members of the class involved.

ANNIE'S ICICLE
(Expressing thought clearly and adequately)

Well, once there was a . . . a . . . nine . . . ninety-nine . . . Once in Denver it snowed ninety-nine feet deep. And, uh, I was out walking that particular day. And, uh, I fell down. And I . . . I needed a stick, but I didn't see one. So I just blew and blew and my breath froze . . . froze into an icicle. And so I picked up the icicle and was on my way.

OPPORTUNITIES FOR TEACHING

It is easy to see that Annie did not do a particularly smooth piece of work. Once she was well launched, however, she never lost her way, nor did she let the bungling start confuse and confound her.

Many ideas were crowding in and each needed to be expressed at the proper moment. Indeed while one thought was being expressed, the next one was in the making. All this was achieved with considerable clarity with pauses only long enough for "uh" and "and." Annie was thinking as she talked.

No one was more prompt than Annie to see the weaknesses of her performance. Listening to the tape recording of her story, her eyes grew wide with surprise. "I loused up the start and I used lots of 'ands' and 'uhs'," she said. "The beginning was not so good as the end," added a classmate. "But did you notice," suggested the teacher, "that Annie connected two ideas very nicely? She did it twice." "I needed a stick *but* I didn't see one" and "I picked up the icicle *and* was on my way."

Annie neither wrote nor outlined her story. She got an idea for a tall tale, thought about it for a while as she gazed out of the window, then rose and shared it with her classmates. It was a spur-of-the-moment experience which lacked smoothness in the telling, but carried the nub of such an interesting idea and was told with such sparkle as to delight the listeners.

Annie's mental bank account had in it a sizable deposit before it was tapped on this occasion. She had read many of the Paul Bunyan stories and a number of fanciful tales encountered in readers; she had listened attentively to stories read and told by her teacher; with the rest of the class she had studied how to tell an imaginary story.

As a result, she had a sense of story form with its beginning, happenings, climax and conclusion, and knew some of the tricks of the storyteller's art, for example, repeating words for effect and holding back the surprise until nearing the end. As for what to tell, her mind was full of ideas.

Miss Mead wanted to encourage this type of spontaneity, but she wanted, also, growth toward smoothness of speech.

Listening to this story and others, she felt assured that further work on rounding out one thought before starting another was needed by all members of the class. Needed, also, was work on the problem of joining thoughts which belonged together, so as to avoid a choppy effect in talking. This would become the content for her language period some time in the near future—forming sentences.

On that occasion, the following conversation occurred.

Teacher: I am sure we have all noticed that when we are talking— telling a story or making a report—thoughts often come tumbling so rapidly that it is difficult to tell where one begins and the other ends.

Children *(laughing):* Yes!

Teacher: What happens then?

Carol: I say "well" and "ah" and "uh."

Edward: And I say "and" too many times.

Teacher: Nearly everybody, even a grownup, uses extra words some- times, but we do need to keep them down. How do you think we can learn to do that?

Ken: By not talking so fast. If we stopped when we were ready to say "ah," maybe we could think of the word we wanted.

Mary: If I piped down, I could separate my thoughts better.

Henry: Maybe if we prepared better we wouldn't use so many "ahs."

Teacher: Listening to other people talk and reading what has been written are two other good ways of helping ourselves. We don't want to run on and on, stringing our thoughts together, and we don't want to make everything we say short and choppy. Suppose I read to you a run-on sentence and you try to change it to something better. Ready?

Children *(heartily):* Yes!

Teacher: I went downtown and John went with me and we were going to buy Halloween masks and . . . .

Henry: I went downtown. John went with me. We bought Halloween masks.

Teacher: Let's hear just the first two thoughts said together.

Susan: I went downtown and John went with me.

Teacher: Could we say that in another way?

Rosa: John and I went downtown together.

This kind of experience went on for some time. Finally, an additional thought emerged and led to further conversation.

Bob: We ought to say our ideas in different ways, not all alike.

Teacher: What do you mean? Give us an example.

Bob: When John and I went downtown, we bought Halloween masks.

Teacher: Can we think of any other unusual way of expressing this thought?

Carol: What do you think John and I did when we went downtown? We bought masks.

This continued for some time until the children had used simple declarative and compound sentences, questions and exclamations; had used a clause and a phrase as well as a subject to introduce sentences; had broken run-on sentences into separate units, making combinations of appropriate parts—without using grammatical terms.

At the request of the children, Miss Mead had transcribed the tape recordings of their stories and made them into a book (p. 30). As a prelude to releasing the collection to the reading table, she now read a selection of well-formed and interesting sentences, as she leafed through the pages:

"The toad tried to tell her, but it wasn't any use because, you see, he was hanging by his tongue."

"He had a long green tail that swished around when he swam."

"He [a "weiner" dog] was so long that it took about five hours to get around one block."

"He [a giant] slipped out and fell in the mud and couldn't get up."

"Especially one day they both [teddybear and rabbit] played together."

"And don't think that's too funny, because Oscar is an ant."

"She [the whale] was wearing a necklace of seashells and bracelets of coral."

Time proved that the children read the stories, and with eagerness. Did they, perchance, grow in "sentence sense" in the process —differentiating the good from the bad, the better from the best?

COMMENTS AND QUERIES

Miss Mead believes that the well-stored mind is the creative one. Acting in the light of this conviction, she worked with her pupils for days in a variety of activities—reading, conversing, studying form —preparatory to this creative moment.

Believing, also, that errors in form can be prevented to some degree, Miss Mead had invested time with individuals and the group on problems that seemed to show the greatest need, such as expressing thoughts clearly and completely (forming sentences).

"Annie's Icicle," as well as many others, showed the need for further study of this problem and suggested a content valuable—for this group—for many a language study period.

In the study period, the teacher used the thought, rather than the grammar, approach. Do you agree with her that grammatical labels can wait until later when they will have more meaning and can be learned more readily?

"Annie's Icicle" furnishes an excellent contrast to "Cats and Mouse" (p. 28) and "Contrary Goat" (p. 89) from the standpoint of smoothness. It bows to neither in ideas or effectiveness in reaching the minds and feelings of listeners.

FAMOUS INDIAN TRIBES

(Developing style)

Attention all palefaces! There were many different kinds of Indians living in the country when the first palefaces came here in 1492. My report is from a bright and colorful book called *Famous Indian Tribes.* The author helped me enjoy this book by writing chapters on Indians and Pilgrims and forest Indians—famous Indians like Little Turtle and Pontiac, plains Indians and their buffalo hunts. The artist has painted large glowing pictures of their country and customs of the Indians. I especially looked and looked at that radiant painting [displaying one in the book]. If you want an action story, you want this book right away.

Using this tape recording with the class was one of Miss Gaynor's techniques for sensitizing children to style. The remarks which followed showed her efforts were not entirely lost.

Sally: He used good words.

Theodore: Some of them were big too.

Pedro: I could hear everything he said.

Nancy: He made it smooth.

Mitsu: He said things different.

Teacher:Yes! Did you notice that he started his sentences in many different ways?

Tim: The first sentence made us all stop and listen.

Harry: Miss Gaynor, where's that book going to be on the shelf?

This and other excellent recordings were used not as models to be copied by all, but for the pleasure they gave and as tuners for the ear. Each child heard his own recording, noted its good points and suggested at least one way in which he might improve.

Miss Gaynor does not limit her children to hearing themselves talk, however well they do it. She keeps colorful and imaginative books on the reading table and frequently reads aloud something which is smoothly written and beautiful to hear. She not only reads; at times, she notes and has her children note words, phrases, and sentences pleasing to the ear, and ways of putting thoughts together so they are enjoyable. Reviews of children's books from the Sunday edition of the newspaper take their place here and help in the setting of standards for reports—not necessarily long, but enjoyable and individual in character.

It is customary in this situation for children to read paragraphs discovered in the study or literature period which have caught their attention and tickled their fancy. Poetry as well as prose has a place here.

Playing with different ways of expressing thoughts helps also.

Teacher: How would you tell me that you made a trip to the zoo and saw a white polar bear?

Nancy: I went to the zoo. I saw a white polar bear.

Teacher: Can anyone say that without starting with "I"?

Mitsu: When I went to the zoo, I saw a polar bear.

This teacher has a way, too, of calling attention to well-chosen words and neatly turned sentences at the time of their occurrence, though she does this without interrupting the speaker.

For moments of leisure, Miss Gaynor keeps a file of folders on a table in the back of the room. In this are to be found a variety of opportunities for independent work—mounted pictures suggesting storytelling; cards bearing words waiting for synonyms; questions asking what words help us to see clouds, hear thunder, feel the wind. Children may talk about these in small groups or use either paper or chalkboard for recording their thoughts.

Miss Gaynor takes pride in her own speech and is not above using a word, now and again, definitely beyond the vocabulary of her pupils, or couching a thought in a sentence form that arrests attention and invites imitation. Her joy comes in hearing the expressions, even if sometimes misused at first, as her pupils stretch toward more effective talking.

Above all, she maintains a permissive atmosphere in which her pupils are free to try new ways of expressing themselves, and to take it as a part of the learning process when they sometimes fail. To keep trying and growing better are goals cherished by Miss Gaynor for her pupils.

COMMENTS AND QUERIES

Noteworthy is Miss Gaynor's individualization of standards. Each child profits by evaluating his classmates as well as being evaluated by them, but in the end each tries to make himself better, not necessarily like the best in the class. How does this differ, from the standpoint of results in personality, from praising only the best and pressuring the least able to attain what is for him, at the moment, impossible?

This teacher achieves remarkable results with the use of the tape recorder in giving children an opportunity to hear how they sound and to make decisions as to ways in which they wish to improve. She eases into the process of recording by the use of small groups in which children speak their ideas to each other and she records only a few ideas in the first attempt.

Miss Gaynor realizes that to teach children to choose words, pronounce sounds and syllables, form sentences, even understand structure and use grammatical terms is not enough for good talking. A child may be perfectly correct and at the same time entirely uninteresting. There is that subtle, somewhat elusive something called style. It is for this that this teacher strives. How well has she succeeded in this instance? How well has she been able to bring style into the concrete by the suggestions she has made and the methods used?

The permissive atmosphere in the classroom emanates from the teacher and bears witness to the fact that she is her own best method of teaching children how to talk—teaching anything, as a matter of fact.

INDIVIDUAL OPINIONS
(Adding labels)

Leader: We're going to talk about the two stories we have just finished. We can compare them or we can say anything we wish about them.

Louis: I think the stories are alike because they show great love for animals. You can tell the author thinks animals should be treated right.

Harold: I think the stories are somewhat the same because both of them show that the author likes animals. One is about dogs and the other about horses.

Sandra: I think they are alike because they are both about animals and about the loving care of animals.

Tatsuo: One of the reasons why I don't think you could tell the author is the same for both stories is because in "Santos, the Horse Hunter," the author plays a character in the story and in "Ginger Follows the Trail" he tells the story as a narrator.

Glenn: Well, I really didn't know they were written by the same author until I saw it at the back of the book, but you could tell the comparison between the stories.

Geraldine: I liked "Ginger Follows the Trail" because it shows a boy heeling a dog on the homeward track.

Patricia: I think the stories are nice because I like the adventuring sort of way the author writes.

Sue: I like this adventure type of story because you never know what happens till you read on.

Mary: Both stories showed a lot of affection for animals and were written beautifully.

Leader: I guess we all liked the stories. I sure did. And that's all the time we have.

OPPORTUNITIES FOR TEACHING

Mr. Radford sat listening to his sixth-grade pupils as they shared their opinions, this morning in early May. His mind went back to September when he received this group of boys and girls—unpoised, contentious, halting, and entirely unoriginal in speech. Sorely tested were his firmly held beliefs that oral language could be taught as used and in connection with all the activities of the school day; that pupils could be motivated by being let in on the problems related to oral communication and by having responsibility delegated to them.

Today as he watched and listened, he saw unmistakable signs of growth in freedom of speech and poise of personality, and rejoiced. He heard ideas, interesting and individual in character, and dared to let himself believe these boys and girls were learning to think for themselves, through language. He noted skills which revealed clarity, not a little beauty, considerable accuracy in form, and felt rewarded for his year's efforts.

Was this enough? The question came with force in the wake of a conversation with a fellow-teacher. The colleague, experienced and effective in many ways, had spoken strongly of the grammar approach to oral language and had summoned an impressive array of favoring arguments—parents want it; children need grammar in order to talk correctly; they have to learn the structure of their language some time and might as well begin now; they need it in order to fit into junior high . . .

Mr. Radford had made a good defense of his point of view—parents want their children to make progress and will go along with the best methods if we can find them and demonstrate their value; knowing grammar does not guarantee effective talking; children can learn the structure of their language later when it has greater meaning for them and is more easily grasped because it attaches to forms and practices already theirs. But what about junior high?

His pupils did not talk about complex and compound sentences, though they used them well; they did not know the parts of speech, as such, but were served by them freely in speech; in connection with errors and approval of well-chosen expressions, they did not give such reasons as "A preposition is followed by the objective case" or "A subject and predicate must agree in number." They merely knew that "for me" sounded better than "for I" and that "boys are" rested more easily on the tongue than "boys is." But, above all, they liked to talk; knew increasingly what to talk about; had a growing sensitivity to appropriate times and places; were moving steadily toward accuracy in form. Was this enough? He thought so, but . . .

On the following Monday, Mr. Radford and his pupils made a long-anticipated trip to the junior high school which most of the boys and girls would attend the following September.

They visited classes, participated in playground activities, toured the building, entered into a social situation where they talked and ate with members of the host group, and came back to their own school flushed with excitement and full of questions.

After considerable gayety in spontaneous sharing of their varied experiences, Edward touched off a conversation which proved to be arresting in character.

Edward: Yesterday when we visited that first class, I couldn't understand what they were talking about.

Teacher: Like what?

Edward: Subjects and predicates.

Teacher *(remembering his wonderment):* That was a lesson in grammar. I thought you might be puzzled. Let me explain. The words are names for forms you have been using in talking. Edward, you had no difficulty in saying a moment ago, "I couldn't understand." You were using a subject and a predicate. The subject was "I"; the predicate was "couldn't understand."

Edward: Oh, I see.

Mary: But what about adjectives?

Others: And prepositions and conjunctions?

Teacher: Let's think about adjectives. Remember the day we talked about a man walking down the street, and you tried to make us see him? What did you say?

Mary: A white-haired, old man.

Teacher: The words that describe the man are adjectives—white-haired, old.

Mary: That's not so hard.

Teacher *(sensing interest and possible readiness):* What would you think if we took some time during the remaining weeks to add a few labels to what we already know about talking?

Children *(unanimously):* Yes!

Mr. Radford, reviewing mentally his approach to language and anticipating the adding of some labels, asked himself again the question, "Is it enough?" His answer, for himself, was an unequivocal "Yes!"

COMMENTS AND QUERIES

Mr. Radford believes in the current trend away from formal grammar in the elementary school to the learning of language through sensitizing the ear to hear words and combinations of words correctly and training the tongue to say what has been heard, leaving the matter of classification of forms and terms for later years. He believes in the possibility of applying labels to what has been learned, granting readiness on the part of the pupils. He does not believe in teaching rules and labels as a means of learning how to communicate.

This teacher was not sure that his pupils were ready for grammatical terms; in fact, he felt sure some of them were not. However, to avoid possible penalization of his pupils who might be judged by their terminology, not their talking, he proceeded to add labels.

Do you approve Mr. Radford's approach to the teaching of language? Do you like his plan for spending the last few weeks in sixth grade orienting children in grammar? If you were teaching in a school which required formal grammar before junior high, could you still make form an outgrowth of usage?

What significance do you attach to Edward's question about grammar, following an orientation trip to junior high? How effectively do you think the teacher handled it? Did he, possibly, ease the sense of apprehension felt and, in its place, instill a feeling of being equal to whatever lay ahead?

To what extent can research help determine teaching procedures? In asserting that grammar does not make the talker, Mr. Radford relied not only on his own experiences, but on the results of studies quoted by Dawson,[6] which fortified him in the belief that his personal judgment stood not alone.

Mr. Radford judges his success in teaching oral language not only on the basis of form but also, and more especially, by his pupils' love for talking and their growth toward effectiveness in expressing their thoughts and feelings. His fondest hope is that his pupils will continue their progress and be eager recipients of any aid which future teachers may give in the interest of talking better and better.

[6]Dawson, *op. cit.,* p. 293.